ARCHIVES OF THE UNITED STATES OF AMERICA

AMERICAN ORIGINALS

By
STACEY BREDHOFF

FOREWORD BY JOHN W. CARLIN
Archivist of the United States

HISTORIAN'S PERSPECTIVE BY DOUGLAS BRINKLEY
Director of the Eisenhower Center of American Studies, University of New Orleans

NATIONAL ARCHIVES AND RECORDS ADMINISTRATION
WASHINGTON, DC

In association with

THE UNIVERSITY OF WASHINGTON PRESS
SEATTLE AND LONDON

PUBLISHED BY THE NATIONAL ARCHIVES TRUST FUND BOARD
AND THE UNIVERSITY OF WASHINGTON PRESS

COPYRIGHT © 2001 BY THE UNIVERSITY OF WASHINGTON PRESS

PRINTED IN HONG KONG

LIBRARY OF CONGRESS CATALOGING-IN-PUBLICATION DATA

BREDHOFF, STACEY

 AMERICAN ORIGINALS/ BY STACEY BREDHOFF.
  P. CM.
 INCLUDES BIBLIOGRAPHICAL REFERENCES.
 ISBN 0-295-98077-X
  1. UNITED STATES—HISTORY—SOURCES—EXHIBITIONS. 2. UNITED STATES.
NATIONAL ARCHIVES AND RECORDS ADMINISTRATION—EXHIBITIONS. I. TITLE.

E173 .B835 2001
973—DC21

                00-064734

Note: THE ITEMS REPRODUCED IN THIS BOOK, EXCEPT WHERE NOTED, WERE SELECTED FROM
THE HOLDINGS OF THE NATIONAL ARCHIVES AND RECORDS ADMINISTRATION. THEY ARE
PRESENTED, GENERALLY, IN CHRONOLOGICAL ORDER AND ARE IDENTIFIED BY RECORD GROUP
NUMBER AND NAME. UNLESS OTHERWISE STATED, THEY ARE HOUSED IN THE WASHINGTON,
DC, AREA, EITHER AT THE NATIONAL ARCHIVES AT COLLEGE PARK, MARYLAND, OR IN THE
NATIONAL ARCHIVES BUILDING IN WASHINGTON, DC.

DESIGNED BY SERENE FELDMAN WERBLOOD
NATIONAL ARCHIVES AND RECORDS ADMINISTRATION

THE PAPER USED IN THIS PUBLICATION MEETS THE MINIMUM REQUIREMENTS OF THE
AMERICAN NATIONAL STANDARDS FOR PERMANENCE OF PAPER FOR PRINTED LIBRARY
MATERIALS Z39.48-1992.

Cover: NORTH FACADE OF THE NATIONAL ARCHIVES BUILDING, WASHINGTON, DC
PHOTOGRAPH BY CAROL M. HIGHSMITH

A DECLARATION
BY THE REPRESENTATIVES OF THE
UNITED STATES OF AMERICA,
IN GENERAL CONGRESS ASSEMBLED.

WHEN in the Courfe of human Events, it becomes neceffary for one People to diffolve the Political Bands which have connected them with another, and to affume among the Powers of the Earth, the feparate and equal Station to which the Laws of Nature and of Nature's God entitle them, a decent Refpect to the Opinions of Mankind requires that they fhould declare the caufes which impel them to the Separation.
We hold thefe Truths to be felf-evident, that all Men are created equal, that they are endowed by their Creator with certain unalienable Rights, that among thefe are Life, Liberty, and the Purfuit of Happinefs--That to fecure thefe Rights, Governments are inftituted among Men, deriving their juft Powers from the Confent of the Governed, that whenever any Form of Government becomes deftructive of thefe Ends, it is the Right of the People to alter or to abolifh it, and to inftitute new Government, laying its Foundation on fuch Principles, and organizing

CONTENTS

CONTENTS

F O R E W O R D

By John W. Carlin, *Archivist of the United States*

For more than a half-century, millions of visitors from all over the nation and the world have entered the Rotunda of the National Archives Building in Washington, DC, to see the original American Charters of Freedom—the Declaration of Independence, the U.S. Constitution, and the Bill of Rights. But we at the National Archives and Records Administration also preserve many other documentary treasures. And we provide access to them as well, through our reference rooms, exhibit halls, nationwide facilities, and web site.

Among these is a critically acclaimed exhibit we opened in Washington in December 1995 entitled "American Originals," which contained a selection of the nation's most significant and compelling documents, drawn exclusively from the voluminous holdings of our archives. From time to time we changed the exhibit's content, for conservation reasons as well as to expand the range of great records available for public viewing. And we have expanded public access to "American Originals" in additional ways.

We have prepared a traveling version of "American Originals" to tour the nation. And we are publishing this catalog.

The traveling version of the exhibit provides a once-in-a-lifetime opportunity for Americans to see a selection of our greatest documentary treasures outside the nation's capital. Not since 1949, when the Freedom Train took documents across the country, has a comparable collection of treasured and historically significant documents been brought together to travel nationwide.

This catalog contains a sampling of the documents shown in the earlier versions of "American Originals" and in the traveling exhibition. It provides a kaleidoscopic view of the national experience—covering the famous and the infamous—as documented in our vast holdings.

The National Archives and Records Administration is proud to identify, preserve, and provide ready access to essential evidence—records that document the rights of citizens and the actions of Federal officials as well as the national experience. The people of a democratic republic must have access to such records to assert their entitlements, hold Government officials accountable, and evaluate the events of their history. Therefore, we invite you to enjoy the contents of this volume not only as a collection of past treasures, but also as an aid to understanding and reflecting upon the meaning of history.

HISTORIAN'S PERSPECTIVE

By Douglas Brinkley, *Director of the Eisenhower Center of American Studies, University of New Orleans*

FIRST-HAND HISTORY

And the rocket's red glare, the bombs bursting in air,
Gave proof through the night that our flag was still there.

FRANCIS SCOTT KEY, "THE STAR-SPANGLED BANNER," 1814

Growing up along the banks of the Maumee River in north western Ohio put American history in front of me at an early age. The War of 1812, in fact, was pretty much impossible to ignore in my hometown of Perrysburg, named in honor of Oliver Hazard Perry, the naval officer who vanquished the British fleet at the Battle of Lake Erie in September 1813. So palpable was the Commodore's renown that his famous cable to General William Henry Harrison—"We have met the enemy and they are ours"—served as the town's all-purpose motto, shouted by kids in snowball fights on the Fallen Timbers Battlefield and even by cool teens at our October football showdowns with Anthony Wayne High School.

Grand statues of War of 1812 heroes dominated the public spaces of Perrysburg, and in the 1970s, Fort Meigs—known as the Gibraltar of the West after future President Harrison held it against numerous British attacks—was reconstructed to look just as it had in 1813. In school we were taught the broader scope of the war: U.S. fleet commander Thomas McDonough's decisive September 1814 victory at the Battle of Plattsburgh Bay on New York's Lake Champlain and Andrew Jackson's systematic stomping of the British on the plains of Chalmette near New Orleans in January 1815. But it was the attack on Washington, DC, in August 1814, during which the British burned our nation's Capitol and White House to cinders, that left the most indelible impression—in part for how the Declaration of Independence was saved from the flames.

The story actually begins with one of the unsung heroes of the American Revolution: Charles Thomson of Pennsylvania, appointed secretary of the First Continental Congress in 1774, whose primary responsibility was to preserve the young nation's papers for posterity. A close friend of George Washington, Thomson became the master archivist for the United States, for he understood that carefully tending our founding documents was as patriotic an endeavor as firing cannonballs at Redcoats. Thus it fell to Thomson to see that the Declaration of Independence—composed June 11–28, 1776, by Thomas Jefferson and fellow drafting committee members John Adams, Benjamin Franklin, Robert R. Livingston, and Roger Sherman; adopted in Philadelphia on July 4, 1776; and signed by members of the Continental Congress on and after August 2, beginning with the body's president, John Hancock— was never captured by any enemy of its ideas nor harmed by fire, water, sunlight, mildew, insects, rodents, or any other natural foe of the paper it was printed on.

After all, that single, 24-by-29-inch piece of parchment represented the heart and soul of our nation.

Thomson did his job well, and when he resigned his post in 1789, many expressed concern about the safekeeping of the Declaration and the nation's other significant artifacts. No less than Jefferson himself fretted that "Time and accident are committing daily havoc on the originals deposited in our public offices." It took two decades, but in early 1810 Congress addressed the problem by appointing a committee to "Inquire Into the State of the Ancient Public Records and Archives." Its members came to a thoughtful conclusion: that aggressive precautions should be taken to ensure that America's priceless Charters of Freedom—the Declaration of Independence, the Constitution of the United States, and the Bill of Rights—would always be treated as sacred treasures of our democracy and protected as such at any cost. On April 28, 1810, President James Madison signed into law the first phase of establishing a national archives.

The timing was impeccable. Just two years later, in August 1814, a force of 4,000 British soldiers landed in Maryland and marched on Washington, DC, burning down the Capitol, the White House, and other Government buildings before proceeding north to Baltimore—where their failure to take the city and Fort McHenry inspired Washington lawyer Francis Scott Key, who watched the battle from a boat in Baltimore harbor, to write "The Star-Spangled Banner," which would become the lyrics to America's undeniably martial national anthem. But even more compelling to me is the account of Federal clerks boldly smuggling the Declaration of Independence out of Washington to the quiet rural town of Leesburg, Virginia. The British may have been able to destroy the great buildings of America's democracy, but they never got close to its cherished Charter of Freedom.

So it came as quite a thrill in the summer of 1976 when, to celebrate our nation's Bicentennial, my parents took me on a pilgrimage to view the Declaration of Independence at the National Archives in Washington, DC. I can still vividly remember entering the neoclassical building at age 15 and waiting in line with a sense of reverence as we approached Jefferson's masterwork. A tour guide informed us that the Declaration—which looked greenish because of the laminated glass around it—was now protected by an elaborate surveillance system: if anyone dared touch the helium-filled display case, the Declaration would instantly drop 22 feet down into a 55-ton security vault. Hearing that, while gazing upon John Hancock's flamboyant signature, made me realize how important the National Archives truly is to America as the trusted custodian of our awe-inspiring national heritage.

This sense has only intensified over the years as I have become personally familiar with the extraordinary collection of documents housed at the National Archives. In fact, I still can imagine no greater joy for a historian than to conduct research there—where a mere 20 minutes after showing proper identification, heading to the appropriate reading room, filling out a form requesting specific documents from the *Guide to the National Archives of the United States*, and donning white cotton gloves—you can suddenly be holding in your own hands such precious treasures as the original document signed by George Washington appointing the first members of the U.S. Supreme Court; Robert E. Lee's handwritten demand for radical abolitionist John Brown's surrender at Harper's Ferry; the deed Secretary of State William H. Seward signed to purchase Alaska; disgraced President Richard M. Nixon's letter resigning the nation's highest office; or the arrest record of civil rights activist Rosa Parks for keeping her seat at the front of a bus in Montgomery, Alabama. Studying these tenderly preserved documents up close—seeing for yourself how Abraham Lincoln dotted his "I's" or FDR crossed his "T's"—brushes away the dusty abstractions of history and makes America's heritage burst to life at first hand in a way that comes as close to touching the past as you can get.

Unfortunately, not everyone can afford the time to visit the research rooms of the National Archives for a leisurely perusal of its paper treasures. Yet all of these rare items belong to the American people, and that gave Archivist of the United States John W. Carlin an idea: why not make it easier for citizens to view at least a small sampling of this inspiring paper trail by taking a few hundred of the documents and putting them in the Rotunda of the National Archives Building which is visited by 1 million people each year. Hence the historical exhibit "American Originals," which for the last 5 years has brought various National Archives gems to the exhibit cases flanking the permanent display of the nation's Great Charters. Although the exhibit can display only a minuscule fraction of the archives' holdings, what a showcase it has been: the original deed of the Louisiana Purchase of 1803 and the manuscript of President John F. Kennedy's Inaugural Address, along with documents that have passed through the hands of George Washington, Wyatt Earp, Helen Keller, Woodrow Wilson, and Eleanor Roosevelt, among other notables. But what about the millions of Americans who cannot visit the nation's capital? As the National Archives prepared to close the Rotunda for a major 2-year renovation, Carlin had the brainstorm of taking some of the great documents in "American Originals" on a tour around the nation providing a powerful educational experience everywhere the exhibit goes. From 2001–2003 the display will appear in museums around the country; but logistical and budget concerns make it impossible to take the exhibit to all of America's major metropolises.

So what can be done to afford a glimpse of these remarkable historical heirlooms to citizens unable to make it to the traveling museum shows? The answer is the catalog at hand: *American Originals* by Stacey Bredhoff, senior exhibit curator for the National Archives. With painstaking diligence, she has assembled an elegant photographic collection of 120 of the touring artifacts, enhanced by her cogent explanations of the historical significance of each, from the first written delineation of the boundary of New Mexico in 1683 to the cable reporting the fall of the Berlin Wall in 1989. Even a passing glance at Bredhoff's table of contents offers overwhelming proof of America's rush to build itself into a great nation: the Articles of Confederation; accounts of the Mormon migration westward; Abraham Lincoln's Emancipation Proclamation, and the reports of his assassination; Thomas Edison's U.S. Patent No. 223,898; the Zimmermann Telegram proposing a German-Mexican alliance against the United States; details of the launch of the Manhattan Project to develop a nuclear-fission bomb, and much, much more.

Although no reproduction can pack the emotional wallop of an actual historic artifact, *American Originals* nevertheless piques the imagination in a way no secondary source ever could. And now, with the addition of this catalog to libraries across the country, every citizen will have easy visual access to many of the raw records of our nation's heritage.

Just about everyone who reads *American Originals* will find a favorite document that moves them for personal reasons, be it the record of Susan B. Anthony's arrest for illegal voting by a female or General Dwight D. Eisenhower's note on the grim possibility of an Allied defeat on D-day. For me, the highest-impact item is the report of Lt. Col. George Armistead on the defense of Fort McHenry in 1814. Like most Americans, I was taught to stand dutifully at attention whenever "The Star-Spangled Banner" was played at concerts, ball games, public events, and professional gatherings, rotely mouthing its dramatic verses without a thought for the 25-hour battle for Baltimore that inspired Key to scribble them on the back of an envelope while he watched the British fire their 1,500-plus shells. Over the years I've even been so foolish as to recommend that Katharine Lee Bates's bucolic 1893 poem "America, the Beautiful" (set to the music of Samuel A. Ward's "Materna") replace Key's fighting words (set to John Stafford Smith's tune "Anacreon in Heaven") as the national anthem. But when I read Armistead's original report on the relentless British bombardment, written in longhand and reprinted in this volume, it suddenly struck me that if Baltimore had fallen that September 13–14 nearly two centuries ago, it is more than likely that the United States would have crumbled.

That the American flag Key wrote about survived the British assault on Fort McHenry and that the brave citizens who defended it forced England's formidable Royal Navy to retreat—against all odds—marks one of the greatest turning points in U.S. history. Thanks to *American Originals*, my education in the War of 1812 that began 30 years ago in Ohio is now far closer to complete, and I will never hear "The Star-Spangled Banner" thoughtlessly again.

One can ask nothing more from a piece of paper, nor from a book full of them, and this is one collection that truly delivers that kind of inspiration on every page. For anyone who can't visit the National Archives and see the Declaration of Independence under glass or view the billions of documents chronicling the development of our nation, *American Originals* is the next best thing.

September 27, 2000

INTRODUCTION

By Stacey Bredhoff, *Curator of "American Originals"*

RIGINAL DOCUMENTS ARE THE RAW STUFF OF HISTORY. THEY ARE PHYSICAL LINKS TO THE PAST. THE ORIGINAL DOCUMENTS OF THE U.S. GOVERNMENT—THOSE THAT HAVE BEEN IDENTI-FIED AS HAVING PERMANENT VALUE—ARE PRESERVED AND MADE AVAILABLE TO THE PUBLIC BY THE NATIONAL ARCHIVES AND RECORDS ADMINISTRATION. *American Originals* PRESENTS A SELECTION OF THE NATION'S MOST SIGNIFICANT AND COMPELLING DOCUMENTS, PIECES OF HISTORY—THE GLORIOUS AND THE INGLORIOUS—IN ITS MOST UNPROCESSED FORM.

IN TEXTBOOKS, HISTORICAL DATA IS PRESENTED FROM A DIS-TANCE OF TIME, THOROUGHLY ANALYZED AND DIGESTED; EVENTS SEEM TO FOLLOW AN ORDERLY PROGRESSION. A CLOSE LOOK AT THE RAW DATA ITSELF, HOWEVER, REVEALS THE DISORDER AND CONFUSION, THE JOY, PANIC, AND BEWILDERMENT THAT CAN CHARACTERIZE GREAT MOMENTS IN HISTORY. ORIGINAL DOCUMENTS SHOW HOW HISTORY IS, LIKE LIFE ITSELF, FILLED WITH SURPRISING TWISTS AND TURNS, IRONIES, MIRACLES, AND MYSTERIES. THEY SHATTER ILLUSIONS ABOUT THE INEVITABILITY OF HISTORY; THEY RESTORE A HUMAN SCALE TO PEOPLE WHO HAVE BECOME LARGER THAN LIFE, AND BREATHE LIFE INTO STORIES THAT HAVE BECOME NUMBINGLY FAMILIAR.

THE POSSIBILITY—NEARLY INCONCEIVABLE TODAY—THAT THE ALLIED INVASION OF EUROPE IN 1944 WOULD FAIL WAS SO SERI-OUSLY CONSIDERED BY GEN. DWIGHT D. EISENHOWER, WHO COM-MANDED THE OPERATION, THAT HE SCRIBBLED A NOTE, "IN CASE OF FAILURE," RIGHT AFTER HE GAVE THE FINAL ORDER, BUT BEFORE HE KNEW ITS OUTCOME. THE ONLY APPARENT HINT OF NERVES ON HIS PART IS HIS ERROR IN DATING THE NOTE "JULY 5," INSTEAD OF JUNE 5 (*see page 98*).

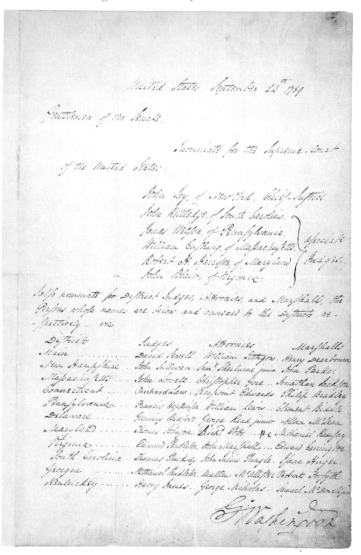

President George Washington names the entire Supreme Court, September 24, 1789

RECORD GROUP 46, RECORDS OF THE U.S. SENATE, REPRODUCED WITH THE PERMIS-SION OF THE U.S. SENATE

Letter from Annie Oakley

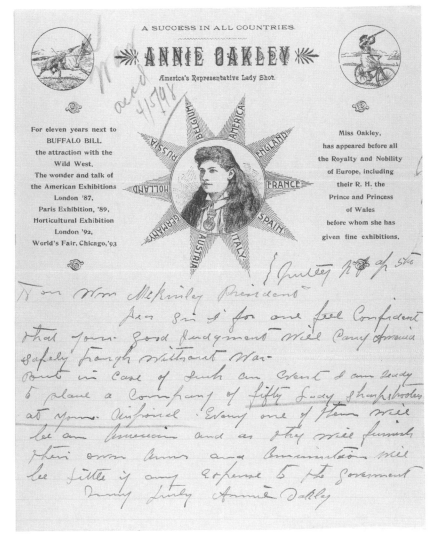

Letter from Annie Oakley to President William McKinley offering to raise a company of 50 American lady sharpshooters in the event of war with Spain, April 5, 1898

RECORD GROUP 94, RECORDS OF THE ADJUTANT GENERAL'S OFFICE, 1780'S–1917

ON JULY 20, 1969, WHILE PEOPLE AROUND THE WORLD WERE TRANSFIXED BY TELEVISED IMAGES OF MAN'S FIRST STEPS ON THE MOON, SOMEWHERE IN THE WHITE HOUSE WAS A STATEMENT THAT PRESIDENT NIXON WOULD MAKE IN THE EVENT THAT SOME CATASTROPHE LEFT THE ASTRONAUTS STRANDED. THIRTY YEARS AFTER THE ASTRONAUTS' SAFE RETURN TO EARTH, THAT STATEMENT IS A POIGNANT REMINDER OF THE UNCERTAINTY THAT ACCOMPANIES ANY GREAT ENDEAVOR (*page 113*).

A DOCUMENT SIGNED BY GEORGE WASHINGTON AMPLIFIES THE MEANING OF BEING THE FIRST PRESIDENT OF THE UNITED STATES: ON SEPTEMBER 24, 1789, ON A SINGLE PAGE, PRESIDENT WASHINGTON APPOINTED THE ENTIRE MEMBERSHIP OF THE U.S. SUPREME COURT—THE CHIEF JUSTICE AND FIVE ASSOCIATE JUSTICES. HAVING FILLED JUST HALF THE PAGE, A CLERK THEN ENTERED THE PRESIDENT'S CHOICES FOR JUDGES, ATTORNEYS, AND MARSHALS FOR 11 DISTRICTS. AT THE BOTTOM OF THE PAGE: WASHINGTON'S CLEAR, BOLD SIGNATURE (*opposite page*).

A DISTRICT OF COLUMBIA POLICE BLOTTER RECORDS THE EVENTS THAT OCCUPIED THE DETECTIVE CORPS ON FRIDAY NIGHT, APRIL 14, 1865: THE INVESTIGATION OF A SUSPICIOUS CHARACTER, THE ARREST OF A 35-YEAR-OLD PROSTITUTE, THE RECOVERY OF STOLEN PROPERTY, AND THEN—ANOTHER SIMPLE LOG ENTRY LIKE ALL THE OTHERS—THE ASSASSINATION OF PRESIDENT LINCOLN, WITH THE NAME OF THE ASSASSIN INCOMPLETE AND MISSPELLED (*page 51*).

THE EVIDENCE PRESENTED AT THE TRIAL OF THE WATERGATE BURGLARS EXPOSES THE DETAILS OF THE 1972 BREAK-IN IN ALL ITS MADCAP ABSURDITY, WHILE THE ONE-SENTENCE RESIGNATION LETTER OF PRESIDENT RICHARD NIXON PROVIDES THE SOBERING FINAL STATEMENT THAT ENDED THE NATIONAL ORDEAL (*pages 118–119*).

THE FINGERPRINT CHART OF ROSA PARKS, REVERED TODAY AS "THE MOTHER OF THE CIVIL RIGHTS MOVEMENT," SHOWS HOW SHE WAS TREATED LIKE A COMMON CRIMINAL WHEN SHE QUIETLY DEFIED THE LAWS OF SEGREGATION ON A MONTGOMERY, ALABAMA, BUS IN 1955 (*page 107*). A 1944 LETTER, AUDACIOUSLY WRITTEN BY AN ADOLESCENT IN CUBA TO THE PRESIDENT OF THE UNITED STATES, OFFERS A GLIMPSE OF FIDEL CASTRO, NOT AS A LEADER ON THE WORLD STAGE, BUT AS A SCHOOLBOY WHO TRIED TO STRIKE UP A CORRESPONDENCE WITH AN AMERICAN PRESIDENT (*page 10*). THE NATURALIZATION PAPERS OF TWO OF HOLLYWOOD'S BRIGHTEST STARS, GRETA GARBO AND CARY GRANT, REVEAL THEM AS IMMIGRANTS MOVING THROUGH A BUREAUCRACY, NOT AS THE GODLIKE BEINGS WE ENCOUNTER ON THE MOVIE SCREEN (*page 96*). THE DALLAS COUNTY, TEXAS, WARRANT OF ARREST OF LEE HARVEY OSWALD FOR THE "MURDER WITH MALICE AFORETHOUGHT OF JOHN F. KENNEDY" EVOKES ALL THE HORROR OF A DAY THAT IS SEARED INTO

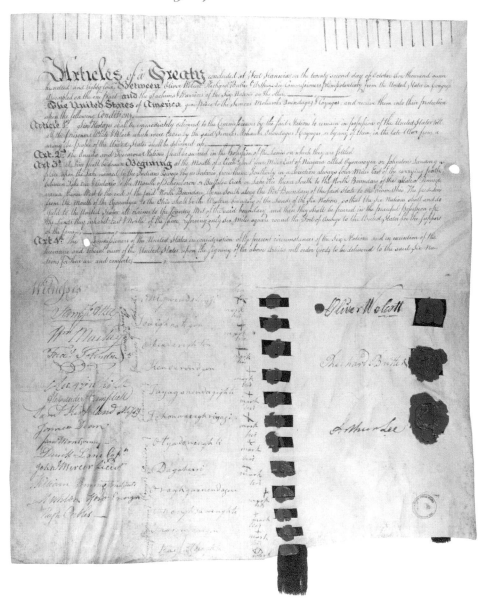

Treaty of Fort Stanwix

Treaty with the Six Nations, concluded at Fort Stanwix, October 22, 1784

Arrest Warrant of Lee Harvey Oswald, November 22, 1963

John F. Kennedy Assassination Records Collection

THE COLLECTIVE MEMORY OF AN ENTIRE GENERATION. THE CAREFUL SIGNATURE OF HELEN KELLER AT THE BOTTOM OF A TYPEWRITTEN LETTER TO PRESIDENT HOOVER SPEAKS AS ELOQUENTLY ON THE MIRACLE OF HER ACHIEVEMENTS AS ANY BIOGRAPHICAL VOLUME ON HER LIFE (*page 83*). THE RUFFLES AND FLOURISHES ON NAPOLEON'S WEDDING ANNOUNCEMENT REFLECT ALL THE POMP AND CEREMONY THAT CHARACTERIZED 19TH-CENTURY DIPLOMATIC RELATIONS (*page 11*).

Original documents hold messages far beyond their words.

THE DOCUMENTS IN THIS BOOK ARE DRAWN FROM THE NATIONWIDE HOLDINGS OF THE NATIONAL ARCHIVES AND RECORDS ADMINISTRATION. THEY ARE HOUSED IN THE GREAT NEOCLASSICAL BUILDING IN THE HEART OF THE NATION'S CAPITAL, IN THE STATE-OF-THE-ART FACILITY IN COLLEGE PARK, MARYLAND, AND IN THE PRESIDENTIAL LIBRARIES AND REGIONAL ARCHIVES THROUGHOUT THE UNITED STATES. THE 10 PRESIDENTIAL LIBRARIES AND 2 PRESIDENTIAL MATERIALS PROJECTS PRESERVE THE PAPERS AND OTHER HISTORICAL MATERIALS OF EVERY PRESIDENT SINCE HERBERT HOOVER. ALL TOGETHER, THE DOCUMENTS OF THE NATIONAL ARCHIVES AND RECORDS ADMINISTRATION NUMBER IN THE BILLIONS AND, IF STACKED IN A SINGLE PILE, WOULD STRETCH 378 MILES.

OF THESE BILLIONS OF DOCUMENTS, THERE ARE THREE THAT ARE SO TREASURED, SO PRECIOUS, SO INTEGRAL TO OUR NATIONAL IDENTITY THAT THEY HAVE BEEN SET APART FROM ALL OTHER ITEMS IN THE HOLDINGS AND DESIGNATED FOR PERMANENT DISPLAY. THE

Letter from Fidel Castro

DECLARATION OF INDEPENDENCE, THE CON-
STITUTION, AND THE BILL OF RIGHTS—KNOWN
AS THE CHARTERS OF FREEDOM—HAVE BEEN
ON VIEW IN THE ROTUNDA OF THE NATIONAL
ARCHIVES BUILDING SINCE 1952. FOLLOWING
THE RENOVATION OF THE ROTUNDA, THESE
DOCUMENTS WILL ONCE AGAIN BE ON VIEW,
RESTING IN THEIR NEW, STATE-OF-THE-ART
ENCASEMENTS WHICH WILL PROTECT AND PRE-
SERVE THEM FOR FUTURE GENERATIONS.

OVER THE 5 YEARS OF ITS EXISTENCE,
THE EXHIBIT "AMERICAN ORIGINALS" HAS PRO-
VIDED UNUSUAL GLIMPSES OF ANNIE OAKLEY,
THOMAS EDISON, GEORGE WASHINGTON, HAR-
RIET TUBMAN, BENJAMIN FRANKLIN, HARRY
TRUMAN, SUSAN B. ANTHONY, ABRAHAM LIN-
COLN, HELEN KELLER, SPOTTED TAIL, RICHARD
NIXON, BRIGHAM YOUNG, UPTON SINCLAIR,
ROSA PARKS, AMONG MANY OTHERS. THEY FIND COMMON GROUND IN
THE HOPES AND DREAMS EXPRESSED IN THE DECLARATION OF INDE-
PENDENCE AND CODIFIED IN THE CONSTITUTION. TAKEN AS A WHOLE,
THEY REPRESENT A GREAT AMERICAN TAPESTRY, ENRICHED AND
STRENGTHENED BY EACH OF ITS THREADS. THEY ARE UNITED BY A
BURNING PASSION FOR LIBERTY—A PROMISE FULFILLED MORE FOR
SOME THAN FOR OTHERS—AND JOINED IN A GREAT AMERICAN ENTER-
PRISE TO FIND A BETTER WAY, TO MAKE A BETTER LIFE. IT IS THAT SPIRIT
THAT GAVE BIRTH TO THIS NATION AND DRIVES IT STILL TO MEET EVER
GREATER CHALLENGES, NONE MORE SACRED THAN THE PRESERVATION
AND EXPANSION OF HUMAN FREEDOM FOR ITS CITIZENS.

American Originals PRESENTS A TINY SAMPLING OF THE REC-
ORDS FROM THE NATIONAL ARCHIVES. IT IS NOT A COMPLETE PICTURE,
BUT A SERIES OF REVEALING SNAPSHOTS. IT REPRESENTS THE LARGER
HISTORICAL RECORD THAT DOCUMENTS THE AMERICAN EXPERIENCE
IN ALL ITS COMPLEXITY. WHILE OFFERING INTIMATE CONTACT WITH
THE PAST, IT ATTESTS TO THE ACCOUNTABILITY OF A GOVERNMENT
THAT LAYS ITSELF OPEN, THROUGH ITS RECORDS, TO THE SCRUTINY OF
PRESENT AND FUTURE GENERATIONS.

**Letter from Fidel Castro, as a young student, to President Franklin D.
Roosevelt, November 6, 1940**
Pages 2 and 3
RECORD GROUP 59, GENERAL RECORDS OF THE DEPARTMENT OF STATE

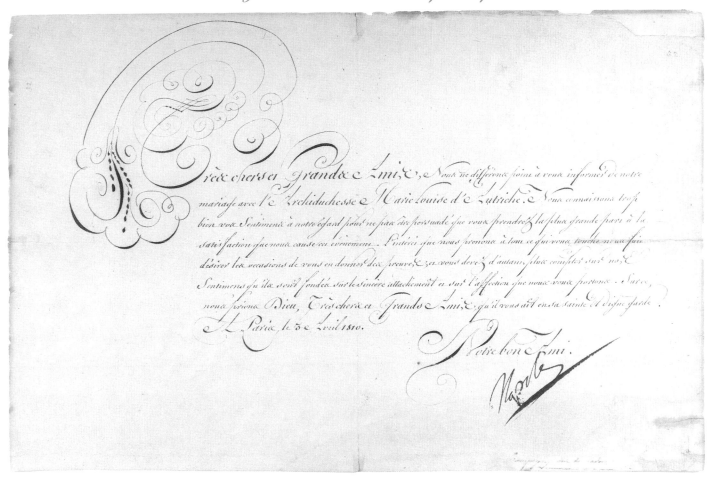

**Marriage announcement of Napoleon, Emperor of France,
to Archduchess Marie-Louise of Austria, April 3, 1810,
received by President Madison**

RECORD GROUP 59, GENERAL RECORDS OF THE DEPARTMENT OF STATE

*V*ast portions of what is now the United States were once part of the Spanish Empire. In a quest for glory, wealth, and adventure, the Spanish explorers, missionaries, settlers, and conquistadors of the 16th and 17th centuries ventured across the Atlantic Ocean to spread the Christian faith and to reap the riches of the "New World."

In 1519, the Spaniards entered the Aztec Empire's capital, Tenochtitlán, one of the world's greatest cities of its day. The glitter of the Aztec gold and the magnificence of the great temples and palaces boasted a wealth of cultural and natural resources. The Spaniards conquered the Aztec Empire in 1521, plundered the great riches of the capital that became Mexico City, and in the following decades, launched a series of expeditions to the north seeking a "new Mexico," in which similar treasures might be found.

Housed at the New Mexico State Records Center and Archives in Santa Fe, New Mexico, is one of the National Archives's affiliated archives, a body of Federal records that includes the land grant records made by the Spanish and Mexican governments. Among them are some of the oldest documents in the holdings of the National Archives.

> *We Americans have yet to really learn our own antecedents. . . . We tacitly abandon ourselves to the notion that our United States have been fashion'd from the British Islands only . . . which is a very great mistake.*

LETTER FROM WALT WHITMAN TO THE PEOPLE OF SANTA FE, NEW MEXICO, JULY 20, 1883

OPPOSITE PAGE:

Viceroy's order setting the boundary of New Mexico, August 20, 1682
First page

In the name of the Spanish Crown, explorers ventured north of Mexico City, claiming dominion over the land and people of what is currently the southwestern United States. They transformed the region forever, imposing a Spanish way of life on the communities whose own traditions in the area traced back hundreds of years.

In 1682, the highest official of New Spain resolved a boundary dispute between the governors of two Spanish provinces—New Mexico and New Vizcaya—setting the southern boundary of New Mexico at the Río de Nombre de Dios, now known as the Sacramento River. This decree is the earliest known document establishing a border for New Mexico.

AFFILIATED ARCHIVES AT THE NEW MEXICO STATE RECORDS CENTER AND ARCHIVES, SANTA FE, NEW MEXICO

Detail from an Aztec Indian drawing, reproduced in *Lienzo de Tlaxcala*, ca. 1550–1564

COURTESY OF THE LIBRARY OF CONGRESS, PRINTS AND PHOTOGRAPHS DIVISION, WASHINGTON, DC

SELLO TERCERO, UN REAL.
AÑOS DE MIL Y SEISCIENTOS
Y SETENTA Y NUEVE, Y OCHEN
TA

1683

Don Thomas Antº Joseph Manuel Manrrique de la
Cerda Henrriquez a fan de Nueraportocarr.º y Cardena Conde de
Paredes Marques de la laguna Comendor de la Moraleja en la Horden y
Cavalleria de Alcantara del Consejo de su Mag.d Camara Junta de
guerra de Yndias Supremo ... Lugar theni... Gouernor y Cap.n Gen de esta
nueua españa y Presidente de la R.l Audiencia de Ella

Por thener nombrado por Gouernador y Cap.l de las Prouinçias
de la Nueua Mex a el Por Domingo Yronsa Petriz de Cruzatte y ha
verse resuelto en Junta General Ser neçessario y Combeniente que
para la facultad que el que... dicho tengo conçedida de repartimientos
de tierras es neçessario se haga Nottorio al Gouernador de la Vizcaya
para que se contenga en las que por su Juridizion solo se le trae para que reçipro...
mente Vno y otro tengan buena correspondençia Conteniendose Cada
Vno en los limittes de su Juridizion asurtandose a las demarcaçiones de
aquellos Gouiernos Contendiendose que la de la Vizcaya Corre hasta el
Rio del Hombre de Dios, ô el llamado Sacramentto y que desde
aqui se empieza el distritto del Gouierno de la Nueua Mexico
Con cuia declaraçion Sesaran las diferençias = Por el presente
Mando al dicho Capittan Don Domingo Yronsa Petriz de Cruzatte
Guttierez haga Nottoria esta resoluçion a Don Bartholome estrada
Cavallero del Horden de Santiago Gouernador y Capitan General del
el Reino de la Nueua Vizcaya para que si tubiere que representar
lo haga ante su superior Gouierno Conteniendose en el ynterim
He Hordenado al que... dicho que todos los españoles que del
Parage del Passo y demas Juridiçiones de la Prouinçia de la
Nueua Mex que Huvieren Hecho fuga y estender
el distritto de su Gouierno los Compella y Apremie

[
Slavery is the great and foul stain upon the North American Union.

DIARY OF JOHN QUINCY ADAMS, FEBRUARY 24, 1820

Sworn statement of Charles Barham, crew member of the *Charles*, July 21, 1685
Signature page

The pink *Charles* (the term "pink" refers to a small vessel) was seized in Long Island Sound for smuggling African slaves into the British colonies. Barham's statement describes a typical voyage of a 17th-century slave vessel: departing from the home port, arriving in Africa (where the *Charles* "received one hundred & forty six Negroes on board"), crossing the Atlantic, landing first in Barbados, and then continuing on to New York and Connecticut.

Barham's account is filled with details about the crewmen, the ship's itinerary, and the cargo on board but only hints at the human horrors of the transatlantic voyage in which loss of life was accepted as a matter of course. He testified that 2 of the crewmen died before reaching Africa, and at least 14 of the Africans died at sea. Profit was the supreme consideration of the Atlantic crossing.

RECORD GROUP 21, RECORDS OF DISTRICT COURTS OF THE UNITED STATES, NATIONAL ARCHIVES AND RECORDS ADMINISTRATION–NORTHEAST REGION (NEW YORK CITY)

In the 16th and 17th centuries, the Atlantic slave trade—the buying, transporting, and selling of human beings from Africa—was the world's largest international business. England, France, Spain, and Holland, the world's superpowers, competed to control the market. Shippers from these nations would arrive on the west coast of Africa with European goods that they would barter for gold, ivory, and slaves.

By the end of the 17th century, the English were emerging as the world's foremost slave traders. In 1672 the King of England granted a monopoly to the Royal African Company prohibiting any British subject outside of that company, from importing slaves to the New World. In 1685 the *Charles*, a British vessel carrying 146 Africans, was seized for violating these British trade restrictions. Documents from this incident provide a glimpse into the vast, global enterprise that supplied slave labor to the British colonies, allowing a system of slavery to take deep root in the fabric of what would become the United States.

Slaves below deck of the *Albanez*, not dated
Watercolor by Francis Meynell

©NATIONAL MARITIME MUSEUM, LONDON

Mizin A Mizin Bonnett a new maine
Bonnett Wanting A bolt Rope; A
basskett of Shackles. And further
Sayeth that all those Comeing in to this
Coast of N: Yorke they brought in Clowon
English men three Dutch men and One Scotch
men. All of them belonging to the shipp
Company:—

Jurat 21° July 84   Charles Barkum

Tho: Dongan

John Willson Aged twenty foure yeares or
thereabouts Marrinor on board of the
Emile Charles Rob.t Codonham Ma.r
being Examined Declareth upon oath that
the Aforesaid Deponicõn is true

Jurat 21° July 84   The ✚ marke
                                          of John Willson

Tho: Dongan

> *We mutually pledge to each other our Lives, our Fortunes and our sacred Honor.*

CLOSING PHRASE OF THE DECLARATION OF INDEPENDENCE, JULY 4, 1776

Assembly Room, Pennsylvania State House, later named Independence Hall, meeting place of the Second Continental Congress

While none of the signers of the Declaration was actually tried for treason, 15 had their homes destroyed, 4 were taken captive, and 1 spent the winter of 1776 in the woods pursued by British soldiers who had burned his home. Before the end of the Revolution, more than half of the delegates to the Continental Congresses suffered direct, personal consequences for their support of American independence.

COURTESY OF INDEPENDENCE NATIONAL HISTORICAL PARK, PHILADELPHIA, PENNSYLVANIA

The decision of the American colonies to separate from Great Britain was a radical move—tantamount to treason—and it came slowly. The proposal for independence in 1776 followed a decade of repeated efforts on the part of the colonists to defend their rights as English subjects. Only when it became clear that the mother country would not acquiesce did the colonists resort to armed conflict and separation. As the men of the Continental Congress moved inexorably toward independence, they recognized that the move constituted an act of high treason against the Crown, punishable by death.

The members of the Second Continental Congress were, for the most part, prosperous and well educated. When they voted for independence on July 2 and adopted the Declaration of Independence 2 days later, they had everything to lose—their wealth, their freedom, and their lives.

🍃 *The holdings of the National Archives and Records Administration include the papers of the Continental Congress, the official records of the pre-Federal Government of the United States. The papers, consisting of about 50,000 documents (170,000 manuscript pages), were created or received from 1774 to 1789.*

Adoption of the resolution calling for independence, July 2, 1776

This document records the July 2, 1776, vote in which the Continental Congress agreed to independence. The words of the resolution, originally proposed by Virginia delegate Richard Henry Lee, are echoed in the Declaration of Independence.

The bottom half of the document lists the 12 colonies that voted "aye" for independence on July 2, 1776. The 13th colony, New York, abstained, awaiting approval from the newly elected New York Convention.

RECORD GROUP 360, RECORDS OF THE CONTINENTAL AND CONFEDERATION CONGRESSES AND THE CONSTITUTIONAL CONVENTION

First printing of the Declaration of Independence, produced during the night of July 4-5, 1776

The Declaration was a stirring call to throw off the bonds of tyranny. This revolutionary document expressed an abiding faith in humanity and political ideals to which this nation still aspires. The Declaration of Independence has been called the birth certificate of the United States, and it is its adoption that Americans celebrate each year with fireworks on the Fourth of July.

The first printed copies of the Declaration of Independence were delivered to the Congress on July 5. This one was inserted into the "rough journal" of the Continental Congress in the July 4 entry.

The official, record copy of the Declaration of Independence, which was signed by the delegates to the Continental Congress on August 2, 1776, is enshrined and on permanent display along with the Constitution and Bill of Rights in the Rotunda of the National Archives.

RECORD GROUP 360, RECORDS OF THE CONTINENTAL AND CONFEDERATION CONGRESSES AND THE CONSTITUTIONAL CONVENTION

The history of the American colonial mail system is the story of the American Revolution. In the British colonies of North America the King's postal service was the only official instrument of long-distance communication. As quarrels between the colonists and the King increased and intensified, the British postal service came to be viewed more and more as an instrument of British suppression and control. Letters between colonists serving on secret committees could be opened and stopped; newspapers, the only mass media of the time, could be stopped or delayed if their messages were abhorrent to the British postal authorities.

At least 6 months before the adoption of the Declaration of Independence, the colonists established their own postal service to secure the channels of communication. The new mail system was both a symbol and an agent in the revolutionary independence movement.

> *Neither snow, nor rain, nor heat, nor gloom of night stays these couriers from the swift completion of their appointed rounds.*

INSCRIPTION ON THE MAIN POST OFFICE, NEW YORK CITY, ADAPTED FROM HERODOTUS, CA. 484 B.C.

FRANKLIN'S POST-RIDER.

"Post-rider" woodcut which appeared on a circular issued by Benjamin Franklin in 1775

Post riders, carrying mail packets in locked saddlebags, traveled at an estimated speed of 12 miles an hour.

COURTESY OF THE LIBRARY OF CONGRESS, PRINTS AND PHOTOGRAPHS DIVISION, WASHINGTON, DC

"The Ledger of Doctor Benjamin Franklin, Postmaster General, 1776"

Benjamin Franklin was appointed by the Crown to serve as Deputy Postmaster General of the colonies in 1753. Although he was directly responsible for many improvements in the colonial postal system, he was fired in 1774 for his pro-colonial activities which were considered disloyal to the King.

With the creation of a mail service independent of the King, the Continental Congress named Franklin as its Postmaster General on July 26, 1775. This account book is a compilation of the financial reports that each of the colonial post offices made to the Postmaster General.

RECORD GROUP 28, RECORDS OF THE POST OFFICE DEPARTMENT

On June 15, 1775, the Continental Congress unanimously elected George Washington to be Commander-in-Chief of the Continental Army—of all the forces raised or to be raised in defense of American liberty. He was not only a veteran of the French and Indian War but a person of unchallenged character. He was a natural-born leader, and his commanding personality lent prestige and legitimacy to the American cause.

In accepting command of the Continental Army, he rejected the $500 monthly salary, refusing to profit personally from the position. It was a widely praised gesture that reinforced the themes of personal sacrifice and patriotism that would resonate throughout his career. He did, however, keep an account of his expenses so that the Government could one day reimburse him.

[*From the day I enter upon the command of the American armies, I date my fall, and the ruin of my reputation.*

GEORGE WASHINGTON TO PATRICK HENRY, 1775

... G. Washington ... Cr (50)

	Doll^rs	Lawful		
By amount bro.^t form.^d	160,074	6450	7	—
By Bal.^ce due G. Washington — & carr.^d to acc.^t folio 65.	——	620	8	4
	160,074	7070	15	4

Note, Before these Acc.^ts are finally closed, Justice and propriety call upon me to signify, that there are Persons within the British Lines — if they are not dead or removed, who have a claim upon the Public under the strongest assurances of Compensation from me, for their Services in conveying me private Intelligence; and which, when exhibited, I shall think myself in honor bound to pay. —

Why these claims have not made their appearance 'ere this, unless from one of the causes abovemention'd — or from a inclination in them to come forth till the force is entirely removed from the United States, I know not — But I have thought it an incumbent duty on me to bring the matter to view that it may be held in remembrance in case such claims should hereafter appear. G:W———n

George Washington's account of expenses while Commander-in-Chief of the Continental Army, 1775–83

Pages 49–50
_The double columns correspond to two currencies—
that of the colony in which the expense was made and
pounds sterling._

George Washington was always meticulous with his finances. In managing his beloved Mount Vernon estate, he accounted for every penny spent, and he applied the same exactitude in commanding the Continental Army.

Throughout the 8 years of the Revolutionary War, Washington kept, in excruciating detail, a complete list of all headquarters expenses he incurred as Commander-in-Chief. This book is written almost entirely in his own hand and includes the charges of blacksmiths, housekeepers, and spies.

Based on these accounts, Washington calculated that he had incurred expenses totaling $160,074. After careful examination of these same accounts, the U.S. Treasury determined that he had underestimated the total figure by $89/90$ of a dollar.

RECORD GROUP 56, GENERAL RECORDS OF THE DEPARTMENT OF THE TREASURY

_The two pages of the volume shown here were photographed
separately, then joined to form a single image._

Benedict Arnold, 1780
Engraving by Benoit Louis Prevost after
Pierre Eugène Du Simitière

Courtesy of the National Portrait Gallery, Smithsonian
Institution, Washington, DC

[*Judas sold only one man.*
Arnold three millions.

BENJAMIN FRANKLIN DESCRIBING THE TREACHERY OF
BENEDICT ARNOLD, MAY 14, 1781

In the early years of America's struggle for independence, Benedict Arnold seemed destined to be remembered as one of the Revolution's greatest military heroes. He impressed his Commander-in-Chief, George Washington, with a tactical brilliance and a genius for inspiring men to fight to the very ends of their endurance. It was his heroics in the early years of the Revolutionary War that made his subsequent betrayal so shocking.

In February 1777, Congress passed over Arnold for a promotion, leaving him angry and disgraced. Though court-martialed in 1779 and formally reprimanded for the misuse of his public office, Arnold retained the confidence and loyalty of General Washington. One month after Washington appointed him commander of the fort and garrisons at West Point, New York, Arnold secretly offered it up to the British at a price of 20,000 pounds. The scheme unraveled on September 25, 1780, when Washington came to inspect the fort and visit Arnold. Expecting to be warmly greeted by Arnold, instead, Washington arrived at West Point, only to learn of Arnold's betrayal. Until that day, George Washington had been one of Arnold's staunchest defenders.

Margaret Shippen (Mrs. Benedict Arnold), 1778
Pencil drawing by John André
Courtesy of Yale University Art Gallery, New Haven, Connecticut

On Board the Vulture
Sept' 25'th 1780

225

Sir,

The Heart which is conscious of its own rectitude, cannot attempt to palliate a step, which the World may censure as wrong; I have ever acted from a Principle of Love to my Country since the commencement of the present unhappy Contest between Great Britain and the Colonies, the same Principle of love to my Country actuates my present conduct, however it may appear inconsistent to the World, who very seldom judge right of any mans actions.

I have no favor to ask for myself, I have too often experienced the ingratitude of my Country to attempt it: But from the known humanity of your Excellency I am induced to ask your protection for Mrs. Arnold from every insult and injury that the mistaken vengeance of my Country may expose her to. I ought to fall only on me. She is as good and as innocent as an angel, and is incapable of doing wrong. I beg she may be permitted to return to her Friends in Philadelphia or to come to me as She may choose; from your Excellency I have no fears on her account, but she may suffer from the mistaken fury of the Country.

I have to request that the inclosed letter may be delivered to Mrs. Arnold, and she permitted to write to me.

I have also to ask that my Cloaths and Baggage which are of little consequence may be sent to me, If required their value shall be paid in money.

I have the honor to be with great regard & esteem Your Excellency's Most Obet. hum. Servt.

Sir Excellency Gen Washington

B Arnold

turn over

Letter to George Washington from Benedict Arnold pleading for mercy for his wife, September 25, 1780

Arnold fled West Point in a panic, just hours ahead of Washington's arrival. Safely aboard the British warship *Vulture*, he wrote this letter affirming his own patriotism and the complete innocence of his young and beautiful wife, Margaret Shippen.

Although she was involved in the plot, Arnold described his wife "as good and as innocent as an angel" and categorically denied any guilt on her part. She bedazzled General Washington and his aides who trusted in her innocence. They allowed her the choice of joining either her family and friends in Philadelphia, or her husband behind British lines. She chose Philadelphia but was banished from there in disgrace and forced to flee to her husband in New York.

It was not until after her death that her full complicity in the plot was confirmed.

RECORD GROUP 360, RECORDS OF THE CONTINENTAL AND CONFEDERATION CONGRESSES AND THE CONSTITUTIONAL CONVENTION

Benedict Arnold's oath of allegiance, May 30, 1778

RECORD GROUP 93, WAR DEPARTMENT COLLECTION OF REVOLUTIONARY WAR RECORDS

I Benedict Arnold Major General do acknowledge the UNITED STATES of AMERICA to be Free, Independent and Sovereign States, and declare that the people thereof owe no allegiance or obedience to George the Third, King of Great-Britain; and I renounce, refuse and abjure any allegiance or obedience to him; and I do Swear that I will, to the utmost of my power, support, maintain and defend the said United States against the said King George the Third, his heirs and successors, and his or their abettors, assistants and adherents, and will serve the said United States in the office of Major General which I now hold, with fidelity, according to the best of my skill and understanding.

Sworn before me this 30'th May 1778 at the Artillery Park Valley Forge

B Arnold

H Knox B Genl

> *The Stile of this confederacy shall be "The United States of America."*
>
> ARTICLES OF CONFEDERATION, ARTICLE 1,
> RATIFIED MARCH 1, 1781

No longer colonies of Great Britain, the 13 states sought a new political identity. The Articles of Confederation, often called this nation's first constitution, defined the former colonies as a confederation of 13 sovereign independent states bound loosely together in a "league of friendship." Reluctant to create a strong central government, the authors of the Articles denied Congress many important powers.

Ultimately, the Articles of Confederation proved inadequate to resolve the political, financial, and social troubles that the United States encountered in its earliest years. However, during the more than five thousand days that the Articles were in effect, there were undeniably monumental achievements: the United States fought and won the War for Independence, negotiated a brilliant peace settlement, created a functioning bureaucracy, and provided for the orderly expansion of a republican form of government into the western territories. The Articles of Confederation were in force from March 1, 1781, until 1789 when the present-day Constitution went into effect.

Articles of Confederation, ratified March 1, 1781
Detail

This document consists of six sheets of parchment stitched together. The last sheet bears the signatures of delegates from all 13 states.

RECORD GROUP 360, RECORDS OF THE CONTINENTAL AND CONFEDERATION CONGRESSES AND THE CONSTITUTIONAL CONVENTION

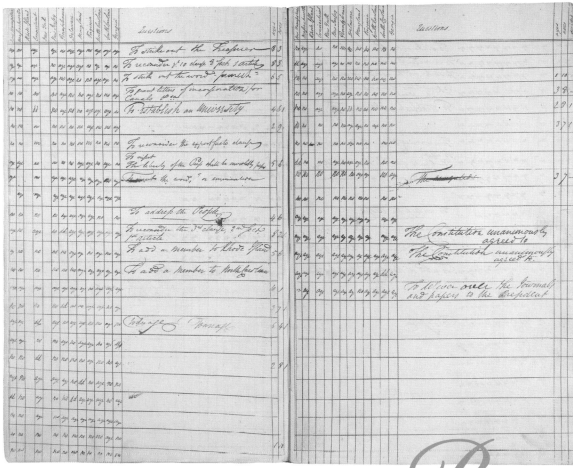

Voting record of the Constitutional Convention showing its final vote on the draft Constitution, September 15, 1787

For 4 months, the delegates debated fundamental questions relating to government, power, and human nature. Each and every issue of the Constitution was painstakingly argued and resolved. The voting records reflect the countless concessions and compromises that produced the Constitution.

William Jackson, who served as Secretary of the Convention, recorded the votes. Throughout the entire voting record, the column for Rhode Island is blank or blacked out, since that state chose not to participate in the Convention. The column for New York is blank only for the later stages of the Convention, as two of the three delegates from that state departed early.

Record Group 360, Records of the Continental and Confederation Congresses and the Constitutional Convention

> *'Tis done!*
> *We have become a nation.*
>
> Benjamin Rush, following the ratification
> of the U.S. Constitution, July 9, 1788

By the beginning of 1787, the American experiment in self-government was at risk of failure, threatened by a variety of escalating problems both at home and abroad. On February 21, 1787, in a climate of economic and political crisis, Congress authorized representatives of the 13 states to assemble in Philadelphia to revise the existing instrument of government, the Articles of Confederation.

One of the first decisions of the body known now as the Constitutional Convention was to carry out its work in complete secrecy. No outsiders were admitted to the proceedings. Although there was speculation as to what the delegates were doing throughout the summer of 1787, there were no public disclosures of their discussions. Under the cover of secrecy the Convention proceeded—not merely to revise the Articles—but to scrap them entirely. The delegates exceeded and violated their mandate, creating an entirely new instrument of government, the U.S. Constitution.

[
*Let the Land rejoice, for you have
bought Louisiana for a Song.*

GEN. HORATIO GATES TO PRESIDENT THOMAS JEFFERSON, JULY 18, 1803

Robert Livingston and James Monroe closed on the sweetest real estate deal of the millennium when they signed the Louisiana Purchase Treaty in Paris on April 30, 1803. They were authorized to pay France up to $10 million for the port of New Orleans and the Floridas. When offered the entire territory of Louisiana—an area larger than Great Britain, France, Germany, Italy, Spain, and Portugal combined (see map on page 28)—the American negotiators swiftly agreed to a price of $15 million.

Although President Thomas Jefferson was a strict interpreter of the Constitution who wondered if the U.S. Government was authorized to acquire new territory, he was also a visionary who dreamed of an "empire for liberty" that would stretch across the entire continent. As Napoleon threatened to take back the offer, Jefferson squelched whatever doubts he had, submitted the treaty to Congress, and prepared to occupy a land of unimaginable riches.

Louisiana Purchase Treaty, April 30, 1803
Cover and signature page

The Louisiana Purchase added 828,000 square miles of land west of the Mississippi River to the United States. For roughly 4 cents an acre, the United States had purchased a territory whose natural resources amounted to a richness beyond anyone's wildest calculations.

The Louisiana Purchase agreement is made up of many documents—some in English, some in French. Shown here is the French exchange copy of one of the agreements regarding the financial aspects of the transaction. It is written in French and bound in a volume with a purple velvet cover. The initials "P.F.," embroidered on the cover, stand for "Peuple Français." The final page of the document was signed by "Bonaparte," first consul of the French Republic and by his foreign minister, Charles Maurice de Talleyrand.

RECORD GROUP 11, GENERAL RECORDS OF THE U.S. GOVERNMENT

The Louisiana Purchase Treaty file also includes the documents written in English that were signed by the American negotiators in Paris and sent to President Jefferson.

Article 15.

La présente Convention sera ratifiée en bonne et due forme, et les ratifications seront échangées dans l'espace de six mois après la date de la Signature des Ministres plénipotentiaires, ou plutôt, s'il est possible.

En foi de quoi les Plénipotentiaires respectifs ont signé les Articles ci dessus, tant en langue française qu'en langue Anglaise, déclarant néanmoins que le présent Traité a été originairement rédigé et arrêté en langue française; et y ont apposé leur sceau.

Fait à Paris le dixième jour de floréal de l'an onze de la République française, ou le trentième Avril mil huit cent trois.

Signé: Barbé Marbois, Robert R. Livingston et Ja.s Monroe.

Approuve la Convention ci-dessus entre et chacun des Articles qui y sont contenus; Déclare qu'elle est acceptée, ratifiée et confirmée, et Promets qu'elle sera inviolablement observée.

En foi de quoi nous avons fait les Présentes, Signées, contresignées, et scellées du grand Sceau de la République.

À Paris le Deux Prairial an onze de la République française (vingt et un Mai mil huit cent trois).

Bonaparte

Le Ministre des Relations Extérieures,
Ch. Mau. Talleyrand

Par le Premier Consul,
Le Secrétaire d'État,
Hugues B. Maret

**Territory of Louisiana ceded by France to the United States
by treaty of April 30, 1803**
Published by the General Land Office, 1933
RECORD GROUP 49, RECORDS OF THE BUREAU OF LAND MANAGEMENT

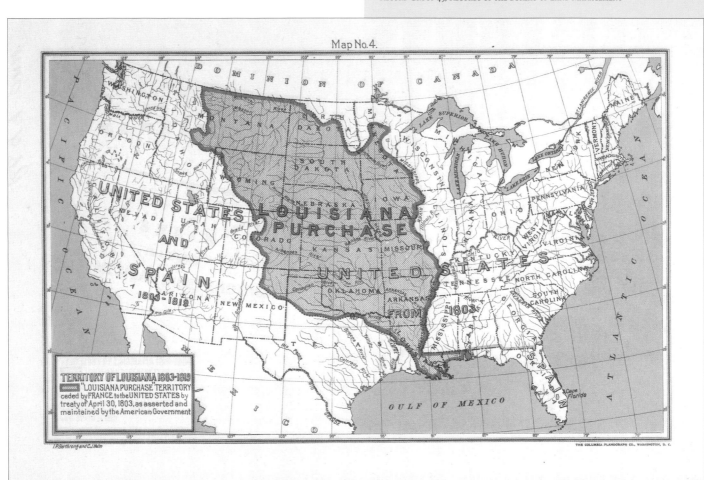

In a secret message to Congress, dated January 18, 1803, President Thomas Jefferson asked for $2,500 to explore the West—all the way to the Pacific Ocean. The modesty of the request, couched principally in terms of promoting commerce, belied the grandeur of the vision behind it. Jefferson had long been fascinated with the West and dreamed of a United States that would stretch across the entire continent.

Jefferson instructed Meriwether Lewis, who commanded the expedition jointly with William Clark, to seek new trade routes, to befriend the western tribes of Indians, and to report on the geography, geology, astronomy, zoology, botany, and climate of the West. The 8,000-mile expedition provided the U.S. Government with its first glimpse of the vast lands that lay west of the Mississippi River.

> *Great joy in camp—we are in view of the ocean—this great Pacific Ocean which we been so long anxious to See.*
>
> WILLIAM CLARK, CO-COMMANDER OF THE LEWIS AND CLARK EXPEDITION, NOVEMBER 7, 1805

TOP: **List of purchases made by Meriwether Lewis in preparation for the expedition to the West, not dated**

MIDDLE: **Receipt for tobacco purchased by Meriwether Lewis for the expedition to the West, June 3, 1803**

BOTTOM: **Receipt for wine and kegs purchased by Meriwether Lewis for the expedition to the West, June 1, 1803**

President Jefferson worked closely with Meriwether Lewis to ensure that he was well prepared—to anticipate what the party would need in the way of arms, food, medicines, camping gear, scientific instruments, and presents for the Indians. They planned well. While the expedition ran out of such luxuries as whiskey, tobacco, and salt, they never ran out of rifles and powder, needed both for self-defense and food supply; and they never ran out of ink and paper, which they used to record their findings.

RECORD GROUP 92, RECORDS OF THE OFFICE OF THE QUARTERMASTER GENERAL

> [*And the rocket's red glare, the bombs bursting in air, Gave proof through the night that our flag was still there.*

VERSE BY FRANCIS SCOTT KEY, INSPIRED BY THE BOMBARDMENT OF FORT MCHENRY, SEPTEMBER 14, 1814

On the night of August 24, 1814, from a distance of some 40 miles, the people of Baltimore could see that Washington was burning. An invading force of British troops had taken the capital, sending the President, Congress, and crowds of panicked citizens into flight. More than 2 years into the War of 1812, with the economy in ruins, the coastlines blockaded, and the capital in enemy hands, the future of the young nation seemed in doubt. The people of Baltimore knew their city was next in line for attack and had been shoring up their defenses for months. The question on their minds that night was not if Baltimore would be attacked, but when.

Three weeks later, on Sunday, September 11, the quiet of the Sunday Sabbath was interrupted by alarms announcing the British invasion. Citizen soldiers, who had stacked their arms outside church doors, raced from their pews to their battle stations. The Battle of Baltimore, a fight that inspired the words of our national anthem, was about to begin.

Report of Lt. Col. George Armistead on the defense of Fort McHenry, September 24, 1814
Page 1 and signature page

The British fleet closing in on Fort McHenry—a garrison strategically located to defend Baltimore from a direct water assault—included 5 bomb vessels (each of which could lob 45 to 50 shells per hour), a rocket vessel, and several frigates. The British were convinced that the fall of Fort McHenry was only a matter of time.

In this report, U.S. Lt. Col. George Armistead described a bombardment that continued, largely unabated, for 25 hours. With the British fleet positioned just out of range, the 1,000 men inside the fort withstood the fiery bombardment. When the British ships moved closer, Armistead let fly with all the firepower he had. By 9 a.m. on September 14, the British Army and Navy were in retreat.

RECORD GROUP 107, RECORDS OF THE OFFICE OF THE SECRETARY OF WAR

spotless integrity in private life — Lieut Russel of the
company under L? Pennington received early in the attack a severe
contusion in the Heel, notwithstanding which He remained at his
post during the whole Bombardment — (Was I to name any
individuals who signalized themselves, it would be doing injustice
to others, suffice it to say, that every Officer and Soldier under my
command did their duty to my entire satisfaction —

                    I have the honor
                        to remain respectfully
                              Your Obedient
                          Geo Armistead
                            Lieut Col? U.S.A.

"A View of the Bombardment of Fort McHenry," 1816

Print by J. Bower

Francis Scott Key, a lawyer from George-town, boarded a British ship to seek the release of an American prisoner and watched the battle from behind the British lines. When Key saw that the American flag was still waving over Fort McHenry on the morning of September 14, he knew the fort's defenders had withstood a night of hellish terror and prevailed. He was so moved by their heroism, he wrote a poem, whose words became our national anthem on March 3, 1931.

The victory at Baltimore that turned the tide of the war and restored Americans' faith in their nation, resonates still, with each playing of "The Star-Spangled Banner."

COURTESY OF THE NATIONAL MUSEUM OF AMERICAN HISTORY, SMITHSONIAN INSTITUTION, WASHINGTON, DC

A VIEW of the BOMBARDMENT of Fort McHenry, near Baltimore, by the British fleet, taken from the Observatory, under the Command of Admirals Cochrane & Cockburn on the morning of the 13th of Sep.r 1814 which lasted 24 hours, & thrown from 1500 to 1800 shells, in the Night attempted to land by forcing a passage up the ferry branch but were repulsed with great loss.

References
A. Fort McHenry
B. Lazaretto
C. Steamer Rose
Admiral Ship · Bomb Boat
E. Ferry and Fort

[
We are men, too.

JOSEPH CINQUÉ, DEFENDANT IN THE SUPREME COURT CASE,
United States v. *The Amistad*, 1841

In July 1839, 53 Africans, who had been sold into slavery on the island of Cuba, followed the lead of Joseph Cinqué in rising against their captors on board the Spanish schooner *Amistad*. They killed the captain and cook and took control of the ship with the intent of sailing back to Africa. Two months later they were discovered by an American revenue cutter off the coast of Long Island where they were arrested for murder and taken into custody.

American abolitionists immediately seized upon this case as a vehicle to display the cruelties of the slave trade and to strike a blow against the institution of slavery. In the lower courts, the chief defense lawyer, Roger Sherman Baldwin, argued that the defendants were free natives of Africa whose freedom had been stolen from them. Their mutiny on board the *Amistad*, the defense argued, was a justified attempt to take back their freedom and return home. This argument served as the basis for the Supreme Court decision which ruled, on March 9, 1841, that all the Africans were free and ordered them released. The *Amistad* incident has remained a symbol of resistance to the 19th-century slave trade.

Of the original 53 Africans captured by Portuguese slave traders and purchased by Spanish plantation owners, 35 survived the ordeal to regain their freedom in the highest court of the American judicial system and return home.

OPPOSITE PAGE:

Statement of Bahoo, a native African, to the U.S. Circuit Court in Hartford, Connecticut, September 29, 1839

Bahoo testified that two of the little girls then held in prison with the "*Amistad* Africans" were native Africans who came to Cuba on the same slave vessel as he did. This was one of several statements that supported the legal argument that the blacks were not slaves but free people of Africa who had been seized.

Bahoo also described the conditions during the voyage: the Africans were chained together, two by two—by hands and feet— throughout the 2-month voyage until they neared Havana.

RECORD GROUP 21, RECORDS OF DISTRICT COURTS OF THE UNITED STATES, NATIONAL ARCHIVES AND RECORDS ADMINISTRATION–NORTHEAST REGION (BOSTON)

I Bahoo of Bandaboo in Africa being duly cautioned depose & say that I knew Marngroo & Kenyu two little girls now in prison at Hartford that they were born in Bandaboo, in Mandingo and came over in the same vessel that I did to Havanna as did Penna and the little boy Carle. That they were about two moons in coming from Africa to Havanna where they stayed less than one moon good many in the vessell & many died were tight together. Two & two chained together by hands & feet night & day until near Havanna when the chains were taken off — were landed on the coast at a little place near sun set stard until night & walked into the city put them in an old building & fastened them in — after some time the people now in jail were put on the same vessel they came here in — in the night and sailed away about the time the gun fired I know these children are the same that came over from Africa and that Marngroo & Kenyu were born in the same place I was which was Bandaboo and further saith not.

Bahoo X his mark

State of Connecticut
Hartford County   Hartford Sept 29th 1839

The United States. App⁵
vs
42.
The Libellants & Claimants of the
Schooner Amistad, her tackle
apparel and furniture together
with her Cargo, and the Africans
mentioned and described in the
several Libels and Claims. —

On appeal from the Circuit
Court of the United States for
the District of Connecticut —
This Cause came on to be
heard on the transcript of the record from the Circuit Court of
the United States for the District of Connecticut and was argued by Counsel. On considera-
tion whereof, It is the Opinion of this Court that there is error in that
part of the decree of the Circuit Court affirming the decree of
the District Court which ordered the said Negroes to be delivered
to the President of the United States to be transported to Africa in
pursuance of the Act of Congress of the 3ᵈ of March 1819; and that
as to that part it ought to be reversed; and in all other respects
that the said decree of the Circuit Court ought to be affirmed — It is
therefore ordered adjudged and decreed by this Court that the decree
of the said Circuit Court be and the same is hereby affirmed except
as to the part aforesaid and as to that part that it be reversed;
and that the cause be remanded to the Circuit Court with di-
rections to enter in lieu of that part a decree that the said Negroes be and are hereby declared to be free and that they
be dismissed from the custody of the Court and be discharged
from the suit and go thereof quit without day. —

March 9. 1841. —

Opinion of the Supreme Court in *United States* v. *The Amistad*, March 9, 1841

Senior Justice Joseph Story wrote and read the decision of the Court. The Supreme Court ruled that the Africans on board the *Amistad* were free individuals. Kidnapped and transported illegally, they had never been slaves. The decision affirmed that ". . . it was the ultimate right of all human beings in extreme cases to resist oppression, and to apply force against ruinous injustice." The Court ordered the immediate release of the *Amistad* Africans.

OPPOSITE PAGE:

John Quincy Adams, ca. 1848

John Quincy Adams, former U.S. President and descendant of American Revolutionaries, repre-sented the *"Amistad* Africans" in the trial before the Supreme Court which began in January 1841. For 8 ½ hours, the 73-year-old Adams passionately and eloquently defended the Africans' right to freedom on both legal and moral grounds, referring to treaties prohibiting the slave trade and to the Declaration of Inde-pendence.

A Mormon wagon train on its way to Utah, 1879

Photograph by W.C. Carter

The Mormon migration was structured, organized, and disciplined. Advance groups prepared the way for those who followed by improving the trail, building cabins, and planting corn. There was a daily schedule for the immigrants, which provided for morning and evening prayer, as well as observance of the Sabbath. The trek did not weaken the bonds of Mormon life but strengthened them.

RECORD GROUP 165, RECORDS OF THE WAR DEPARTMENT GENERAL AND SPECIAL STAFFS (165-XS-7)

arly 19th-century America proved fertile ground for religious fervor and innovation. The first amendment's protection of religious freedom, the promise of a largely unexplored continent, and the rambunctious optimism of a new nation created an atmosphere that gave rise to hundreds of new religious sects that were distinctly American. One of the new religions to take root in American society was the Church of Jesus Christ of Latter-day Saints, also known as Mormonism. Founded in 1830, the Church presently counts more than 10 million among its followers, more than half of them outside the United States.

While the Mormon Church drew large numbers of followers in its early years, it also drew deep suspicion and savage hostility—especially for the creation of a private army and for the practice of polygamy. Seeking sanctuary from religious persecution and driven by what they believed was the direct word from God, the Mormons moved west: from New York to Ohio, from Ohio to Missouri to Illinois, and from Illinois to the Valley of the Great Salt Lake. Trekking across the Rocky Mountains with oxen, wagons, and sometimes just handcarts filled with a few personal belongings, their migration forms a notable chapter in the story of the American westward movements.

There are more than theological reasons for remembering the Mormon pioneers. They were the most systematic, organized, disciplined, and successful pioneers in our history.

WALLACE STEGNER, 1964

Nauvoo (Ill.) Decr. 17. 1845

Sir

As there is a recommend to Congress in the President's Message for a suitable number of Stockades and block houses to be erected between our western frontiers, and the Rocky Mountains. If some one of our people could be favored with the Agency for that purpose we would build them cheaper, then in any otherwise could be done, as we expect to emigrate West of the mountains next season. If we should eventually settle on Vancouver's Island, according to our calculation we shall greatly desire to have a mail route, established between here, and Oregon, we would like to contract for the same through the summer months. When we arrive at the place of our destination we fondly anticipate, we shall have no old settlers to find fault with us and if Oregon should be annexed to the United States, which in all probability will be, and Vancouver's Island incorporated in the same, by our promptly paying the national revenue, and taxes, we can live in peace with all men.

Yours &c

Most Obediently

Brigham Young
President of the Church
of Jesus Christ of
Latter day
Saints

Hon. W. L. Marcy
Sec of War
Washington D. C

Letter from Brigham Young, president of the Church of Jesus Christ of Latter-day Saints, to William L. Marcy, Secretary of War, December 17, 1845

Joseph Smith, the founder and first president of the Church, was killed by an angry mob in Carthage, Illinois, on June 27, 1844. Although he had thought about seeking asylum in the western wilderness of the American continent, it was his successor, Brigham Young, who planned and led the 1300-mile migration that would bring thousands of Mormons to the Valley of the Great Salt Lake.

Young was a brilliant organizer and administrator who masterminded the transplantation of an entire people and a way of life. Trying to raise money for the journey, he wrote this letter to the Secretary of War, asking for a contract with the Federal Government to build stockades and blockhouses between the western frontier and the Rocky Mountains.

RECORD GROUP 92, RECORDS OF THE OFFICE OF THE QUARTERMASTER GENERAL

THE NATIONAL ARCHIVES OF THE UNITED STATES

1

Head Quarters 10th Mily Dept
Monterey, Califa August 17, 1848

No 34..
Sir

I have the honor to inform you that accompanied by Lieut. W. T. Sherman 3d Artillery A.A.A. Genl I started on the 12th of June last to make a tour through the northern part of California, My principal purpose however was to visit the newly discovered Gold Placer in the valley of the Sacramento.

I had proceeded about forty miles when I was overtaken by an Express, bringing me inteligence of the arrival at Monterey of the U.S. Store Ship Southampton, with important letters from Commodore Shubrick and Lieutenant Colonel Burton. I returned at once to Monterey, and dispatched what business was most important, and on the 17th resumed my journey; we reached San Francisco on the 20th and found that all or nearly all its male population had gone to the mines – The town which a few months before was so busy and thriving, was then almost deserted. On the evening of the 24th the horses of the escort were crossed to Sousolito in a launch, and on the following day we resumed the journey by way of Bodega and Sonoma, to Sutter's Fort, where we arrived on the morning of the 2d of July. Along the whole route mills were lying idle; fields of wheat were open to cattle & horses, houses vacant, and farms going to waste. At Sutter's there was

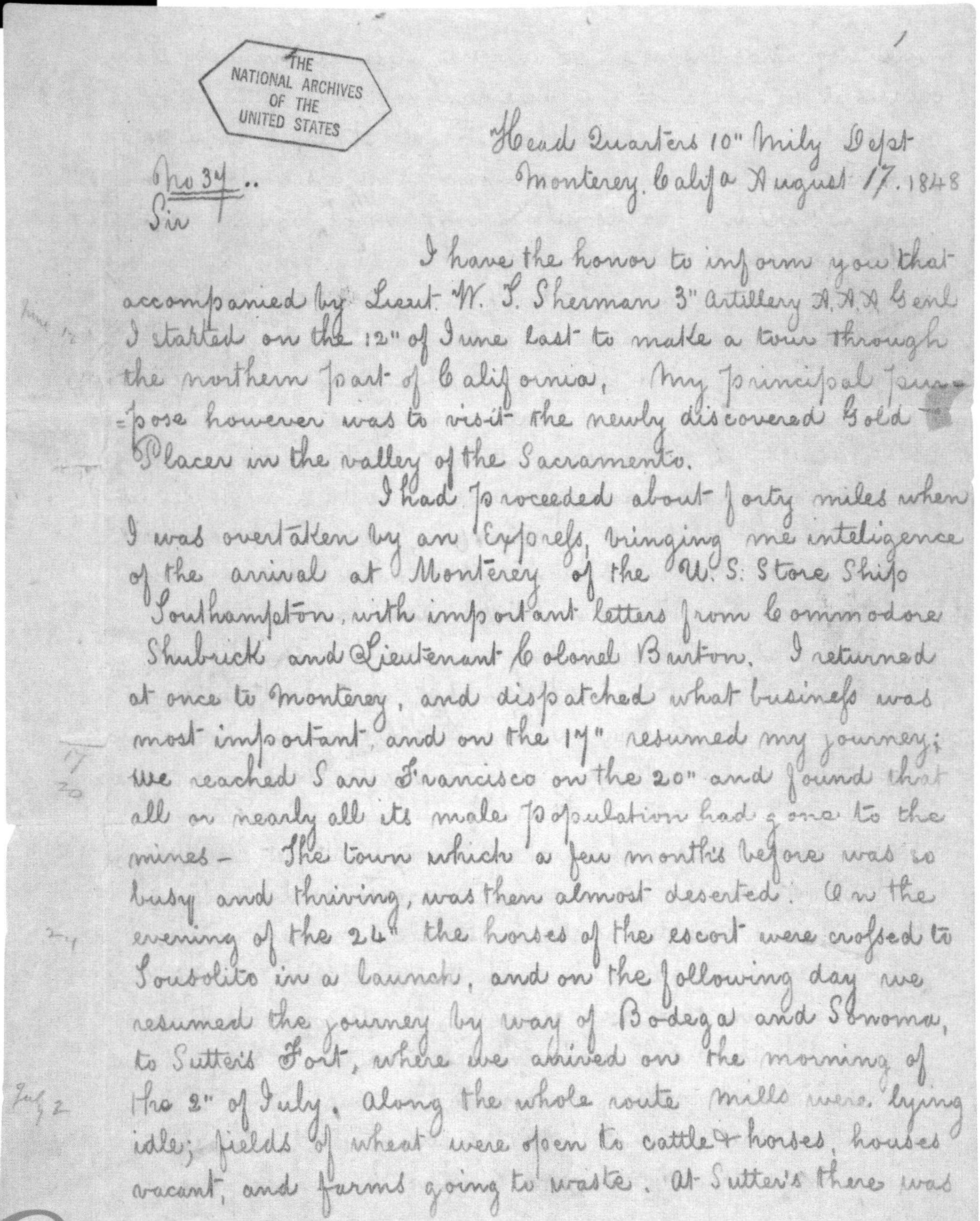

Letter from Richard B. Mason, military governor of California to William Marcy, Secretary of War, reporting on the California gold mines, August 17, 1848
First of 17 pages

Following an official tour of the goldfields during the summer of 1848, the military governor of California sent this report (supplemented with maps and gold specimens) to Washington, DC. President James Polk's public confirmation in December of the gold discovery ignited the rush that sent thousands of people to California.

RECORD GROUP 94, RECORDS OF THE ADJUTANT GENERAL'S OFFICE 1780'S–1917

The documents shown here were part of an official report on the California goldfields delivered to the Secretary of War. The letter is preserved among the military records; the map is one of 2.5 million preserved by the National Archives and Records Administration.

On January 24, 1848, James Marshall discovered gold in northern California while building a sawmill in a joint venture with his wealthy partner, John Sutter. News of this discovery set off a world-wide migration as farmers abandoned their fields, sailors jumped ship, and shopkeepers left their settled lives for the promise of quick wealth in California. People from Peru, Chile, Australia, Hawaii, and Europe joined Americans in a mad rush to the California goldfields.

I believe this is gold.

JAMES W. MARSHALL, JANUARY 28, 1848, 4 DAYS AFTER DISCOVERING GOLD IN THE AMERICAN RIVER IN NORTHERN CALIFORNIA

"Lower Mine or Mormon Diggings"
Map made by Lt. William Tecumseh Sherman,
July 20, 1848

As the military governor's chief of staff, Lt. William Tecumseh Sherman toured the goldfields and prepared maps to accompany the official report. This map shows the presence of gold along the American River where the first discovery was made.

RECORD GROUP 77, RECORDS OF THE OFFICE OF THE CHIEF OF ENGINEERS

[*I John Brown am now quite certain that the crimes of this guilty land will never be purged away but with Blood.*

JOHN BROWN, DECEMBER 2, 1859

The destruction of slavery in the United States was the driving ambition of abolitionist John Brown. He came to believe that it would take bloodshed to root out the evil of slavery, and by the mid-1850s he dedicated himself to an all-out war for slave liberation. On October 16, 1859, he and his "army" of some 20 men seized the Federal arsenal at Harpers Ferry, Virginia (now West Virginia). By the morning of October 18, marines under the command of Bvt. Col. Robert E. Lee stormed the building and captured Brown and the survivors of his party. The operation that Brown envisioned as the first blow in a war against slavery was over in 36 hours.

The fears inspired by the raid on Harpers Ferry exceeded and outlasted its actual threat. For thousands of Southerners, it was evidence of a vast conspiracy of Northern abolitionists whose object was to incite violence and destroy the Southern way of life. John Brown's raid exacerbated a deepening sectional crisis between North and South and brought the nation one step closer to civil war. John Brown was hanged for treason on December 2, 1859.

John Brown, ca. 1850

RECORD GROUP 127, RECORDS OF THE U.S. MARINE CORPS
(127-N-521396)

A.

Hd Qrs: Harpers Ferry
18 Oct 1859

Colonel Lee U.S.A. Command the troops
sent by the President of the U.S. to suppress the
insurrection at this place; demands the surrender
of the persons in the Armory buildings.

If they will peaceably surrender themselves
restore the pillaged property; they shall be kept in
safety to await the orders of the President.

Col Lee represents to them in all frankness
that it is impossible for them to escape; that the
Armory is surrounded on all sides by troops; &
that if he is compelled to take them by force
he cannot answer for their safety.

(Signed) R E Lee
Col Comm
U.S. Troops

Robert E. Lee's demand for the surrender of John Brown and his party, October 18, 1859

When Brown refused to unconditionally accept the terms of this note, Lee gave the order to storm the building.

Part of report submitted by Bvt. Col. Robert E. Lee to the Secretary of War, October 19, 1859

Listed among the insurgents who had died during the raid were two of John Brown's sons, Oliver and Watson.

B.

List of Insurgents

John Brown	of N.Y.	Comm'r in Chief	Badly wounded. Prisoner.
Aaron C. Stevens	Conn.	Captain	Badly wounded. Prisoner.
Edwin Coppoc	Iowa.	Lieutenant	Unhurt Prisoner
Oliver Brown	N.Y.	Captain	Killed
Watson Brown	N.Y.	Captain	Killed
Albert Hazlett	Penn'a	Lieut	Killed
W'm Leeman	Maine	Lieut.	Killed
Stewart Taylor	Canada	Private	Killed
Chas. P. Tidd	Maine	Private	Killed
W'm Thompson	N.Y.	Private	Killed
Adolph Thompson	N.Y.	Private	Killed
John Kagi	Ohio	Private	Killed
Jeremiah Anderson	Ind'a	Private	Killed
John E. Cook	Conn.	Captain	Escaped

Negroes

Dangerfield Newby	Ohio		Killed.
Louis Leary	Ohio, Oberlin		Killed
Green Shields (alias Emperor)	N.Y.		Unhurt Prisoner
Copeland	Ohio, Oberlin		Prisoner
O. P. Anderson	Penn'a		Unaccounted for.

> *Our separatism is final, absolute and eternal.*
>
> LAWRENCE M. KEITT, SOUTH CAROLINA DELEGATE TO THE
> CONVENTION OF SECEDED STATES, FEBRUARY 9, 1861

Although mistrust and antagonism between the Northern and Southern states had long existed, it was the bitter argument over slavery that stretched the bonds of the Union to the breaking point. When Abraham Lincoln, viewed by many as the embodiment of Northern interests, was elected President in 1860, many Southerners felt they had lost control over their destiny. Immediately after the election, seven states of the lower South began the process of secession. By the time Lincoln was sworn in, South Carolina, Mississippi, Florida, Alabama, Georgia, Louisiana, and Texas had withdrawn from the Union.

The states of the upper South—Virginia, Arkansas, Tennessee, and North Carolina—were less hasty. They wavered between Union and secession until it was clear that war was imminent. It was only when Abraham Lincoln assumed office and demonstrated that he would not allow secession—when he issued a call for 75,000 troops to suppress the rebellion—when the people of the upper Southern states felt that they were about to be invaded, that they too voted to secede.

OPPOSITE PAGE:

Ordinance of Secession of the State of Virginia, adopted by the Convention of Virginia, April 17, 1861, ratified by the people of Virginia, May 23, 1861

Two days after President Lincoln issued a call for troops, the Convention in Virginia passed the Ordinance of Secession.

Virginia's withdrawal from the Union was a major coup for the Confederacy and had a profound impact on those states still contemplating secession. The state that was the birthplace and home of George Washington, Thomas Jefferson, and many other heroes of the American Revolution lent both dignity and legitimacy to the Confederate cause, as well as the promise of new talent, both political and military. Within a month, Arkansas, Tennessee, and North Carolina also seceded.

RECORD GROUP 59, GENERAL RECORDS OF THE DEPARTMENT OF STATE

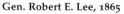

Gen. Robert E. Lee, 1865

Detail

RECORD GROUP 111, RECORDS OF THE OFFICE OF THE CHIEF SIGNAL OFFICER (111-B-1564)

An Ordinance to Repeal the Ratification of the Constitution of the United States of America by the State of Virginia, and to resume all the rights and powers granted under said Constitution.

THE PEOPLE OF VIRGINIA in their ratification of the Constitution of the United States of America adopted by them in Convention on the twenty fifth day of June in the year of our Lord one thousand, seven hundred and eighty eight having declared that the powers granted under the said Constitution were derived from the people of the United States, and might be resumed whensoever the same should be perverted to their injury and oppression; and the Federal Government having perverted said powers not only to the injury of the people of Virginia, but to the oppression of the Southern slaveholding States:

Now, therefore, we, the People of Virginia do declare and ordain that the Ordinance adopted by the people of this State, in Convention, on the twenty fifth day of June, in the year of our Lord one thousand seven hundred and eighty eight whereby the Constitution of the United States of America was ratified, and all acts of the General Assembly of this State ratifying or adopting amendments to said Constitution are hereby repealed and abrogated; that the Union between the State of Virginia and the other States under the Constitution aforesaid is hereby dissolved; and that the State of Virginia is in the full possession and exercise of all the rights of sovereignty which belong and appertain to a free and independent State. And they do further declare that said Constitution of the United States of America is no longer binding on any of the citizens of this State.

This ordinance shall take effect, and be an act of this day when ratified by a majority of the votes of the people of this State cast at a poll to be taken thereon on the fourth Thursday in May next, in pursuance of a schedule hereafter to be enacted.

DONE IN CONVENTION in the city of Richmond on the seventeenth day of April, in the year of our Lord one thousand eight hundred and sixty one, and in the eighty fifth year of the Commonwealth of Virginia.

Angus R. Blakey

Wm H Dulany   John Rand Chambliss   John Janney President
John T. Thornton Geo. Wythe Randolph Geo. P. Taylor   W.B. Cecil   James W. Sheffey
Wm. C. Scott   James P. Holcombe   P.B. Borst   Geo. Blow Jr.   Addison Hall
                  Williams Carter Wickham Samuel G. Staples John Campbell Jeremiah Morton
R.H. Cox   George W. Richardson   Wm H Coffman   Wood Bouldin
                  John Tyler B.P. Grant Wm J. Neblett   Mc Gruder
                  John Goode Jr   John R. Pleasants   Richard H. Duke
                  Edmd. T. Morris   Miers W. Fisher Walter D. Leake William W Forbes
                  Wm. W. Boyd   Manilius Chapman   Lewis D. Isbell
                  James H. Cox   W.C. Sutherlin D.B. McIee Benj F. Wysor
                  John L. Marye   George Wm Brent   James C. Bruce
                  Sam L. Williams   James M. Strange   James Gustavus Holladay
                  Marmaduke Johnson   Nicolas G. Seffield J. ... Lewis E. Harvie
                  James Boisseau   Hugh M. Nelson   Franklin P. Turner
                  J. Mallory   John Richardson Kilby   Wm Ballard Preston
                  A. F. Fraquer   Wm. Campbell Scott W. McComas
                  Thos Branch   Wm H Macfarland R.B. French John Critcher
                  Robt H Turner   Peter C. Johnston Samuel L. Graham Robert C. Kent
                  Wm H ...   Cyrus P. Fisher Wm McKinney Hy M Conn
                  R. M. Cabell   James Lawson A.T. Gray Saml Woods
                  Wm M Reed C.K. Slaughter W.C. Scott   Benjamin Wilson
                  Chas K Mallory   Jno Barbour   Cyrus Hall
                  A. F. Caperton   James B. Dorman   Peyton Gravely

Robert E. Lee's resignation from the Army of the United States, April 20, 1861

The onset of the Civil War forced unwanted choices onto thousands of Americans. One-third of the nation's commissioned military officers resigned their commissions to join the Confederate cause. Robert E. Lee was one of them.

Initially, Lee had opposed secession and viewed the people of the lower South as "cotton-state" extremists. He had devoted his career to the U.S. Army, to the nation, and held out every hope that the Union would be preserved. But when war came, in a decision that caused him great anguish, he cited his first loyalty to the State of Virginia and refused to take up arms against the South. When President Lincoln offered him leadership of the U.S. Army, Lee refused and submitted this letter of resignation to the Secretary of War. Three days later, he accepted the command of the military and naval forces of Virginia.

RECORD GROUP 94, RECORDS OF THE ADJUTANT GENERAL'S OFFICE, 1780'S–1917

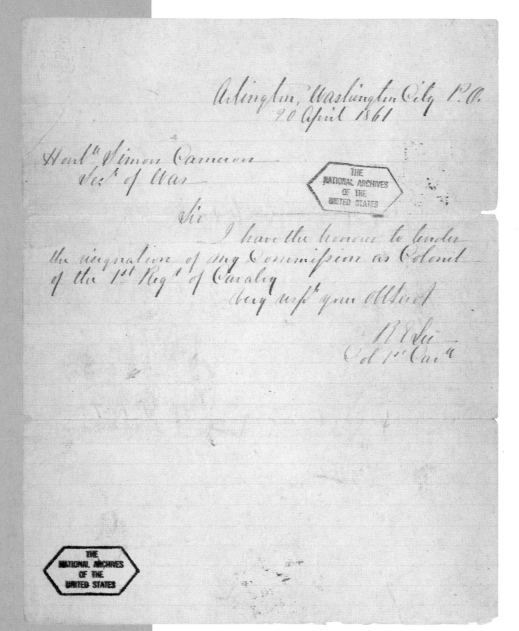

OPPOSITE PAGE:

Gen. Robert E. Lee, 1865

Photograph from the Mathew Brady Collection

RECORD GROUP 111, RECORDS OF THE OFFICE OF THE CHIEF SIGNAL OFFICER (111-B-1564)

> *I cannot raise my hand against my birthplace, my home, my children.*
>
> ROBERT E. LEE, MAY 5, 1861

> *When you are dead and in Heaven,*
> *in a thousand years that action of*
> *yours will make the Angels sing*
> *your praises.*

HANNAH JOHNSON, MOTHER OF A NORTHERN BLACK SOLDIER,
WRITING TO PRESIDENT ABRAHAM LINCOLN ABOUT THE
EMANCIPATION PROCLAMATION, JULY 31, 1863

When President Lincoln needed to concentrate—when he faced a task that required his focused and undivided attention—he would leave the White House, cross the street to the War Department, and take over the desk of Thomas T. Eckert, chief of the military telegraph staff. "I come here to escape my persecutors," Lincoln once remarked. The hub of the Union's military communication center had become an unlikely refuge for the President. Anxiously awaiting the latest reports from the front, hovering over the shoulder of an operator, he would enjoy the easy banter of the telegraph staff and, somehow, find relief from the great strains of his office. In this congenial getaway, amid the clattering of the telegraph keys, the President wrote the earliest draft of the Emancipation Proclamation.

One day in late June or early July 1862, he asked Eckert for some paper, explaining that he had something "special" to write. Slowly, putting down just one or two lines at a time, Lincoln began to work. During the next several weeks, he continued writing in the telegraph office—a little bit each day— charging Eckert with the safekeeping of his papers at night. Only when a draft was finished did Lincoln reveal that he had composed an order "giving freedom to the slaves in the South, for the purpose of hastening the end of the war." The document changed the course of the war and of American history. In its final version, the order was issued on January 1, 1863, and is known today as the Emancipation Proclamation.

OPPOSITE PAGE:

The Emancipation Proclamation, January 1, 1863
Page 1 and signature page

President Abraham Lincoln issued the Emancipation Proclamation on January 1, 1863, as the nation approached its third year of bloody civil war. The proclamation declared "that all persons held as slaves" within the rebellious states "are, and henceforward shall be free."

Despite that expansive wording, the Emancipation Proclamation was limited in many ways. It applied only to states that had seceded from the Union, leaving slavery untouched in the loyal border states. It also expressly exempted parts of the Confederacy that had already come under Northern control. Most important, the freedom it promised depended upon Union military victory.

Although the Emancipation Proclamation did not immediately free a single slave, it captured the hearts and imaginations of millions of African Americans and fundamentally transformed the character of the war. After January 1, 1863, every advance of Federal troops expanded the domain of freedom. Moreover, the proclamation announced the acceptance of black men into the Union army and navy, enabling the liberated to become liberators. By the end of the war, almost 200,000 black soldiers and sailors had fought for the Union and freedom.

From the first days of the Civil War, slaves had acted to secure their own liberty. The Emancipation Proclamation confirmed their insistence that the war for the Union must become a war for freedom. It added moral force to the Union cause and strengthened the Union both militarily and politically. Along the road to slavery's final destruction, the Emancipation Proclamation has assumed a place among the great documents of human freedom.

RECORD GROUP 11, GENERAL RECORDS OF THE U.S. GOVERNMENT

one thousand eight hundred
and sixty three, and of the
Independence of the United
States of America the eighty-
seventh.

Abraham Lincoln

By the President:

William H. Seward
Secretary of State.

By the President of the United States of America:

A Proclamation.

Whereas, on the twenty-second day of
September, in the year of our Lord one thousand
eight hundred and sixty-two, a proclamation
was issued by the President of the United States,
containing, among other things, the following,
to wit:

"That on the first day of January, in the
"year of our Lord one thousand eight hundred
"and sixty-three, all persons held as slaves within
"any State or designated part of a State, the people
"whereof shall then be in rebellion against the
"United States, shall be then, thenceforward, and
"forever free; and the Executive Government of the
"United States, including the military and naval
"authority thereof, will recognize and maintain
"the freedom of such persons, and will do no act
"or acts to repress such persons, or any of them,
"in any efforts they may make for their actual
"freedom.

"That the Executive will, on the first day

Civil War general Ulysses S. Grant earned the nickname "Unconditional Surrender" Grant after his 1862 victory at Fort Donelson in Tennessee. For his proven military skills and for his bulldog determination to destroy the Confederate armies, President Lincoln picked Grant in March 1864 to be Lieutenant General of the U.S. Army—commander of all Union forces. In June of that year, Grant set out to capture Petersburg, Virginia, the hub of a railroad system that carried food and supplies to the Confederate capital city of Richmond and to Gen. Robert E. Lee's army. Although the Union's initial assaults failed to capture the city, they did sever some of these railroad lines. By July both Confederate and Union forces were dug in for a long, slow battle of attrition.

The Confederates' condition steadily deteriorated as Grant attempted to cut off their lifeline of supplies, while the Union forces enjoyed a constant stream of food, men, and armaments. The grim siege, which took place in a snakelike system of trenches, lasted nearly 10 months, ending just days before Lee surrendered his army to Grant.

Hold on with a bull-dog grip, and chew & choke, as much as possible.

PRESIDENT ABRAHAM LINCOLN TO LT. GEN. ULYSSES S. GRANT, DURING THE SIEGE AT PETERSBURG, VIRGINIA, AUGUST 17, 1864

Telegram from President Lincoln to Lieutenant General Grant, August 17, 1864

In August 1864 Grant protested a proposal that some of his troops be removed from Petersburg, arguing that it would weaken his hold on the city. The President agreed and sent this message to Grant offering words of encouragement.

RECORD GROUP 107, RECORDS OF THE OFFICE OF THE SECRETARY OF WAR

Confederate Trenches, Petersburg, Virginia, not dated
Photograph from the Mathew Brady Collection

Shown here is one small section of the trenches that circled the city of Petersburg during the siege of 1864. The entrenchments at Petersburg foreshadowed the style of warfare that would characterize much of the fighting during World War I.

RECORD GROUP 111, RECORDS OF THE OFFICE OF THE CHIEF SIGNAL OFFICER (111-B-372)

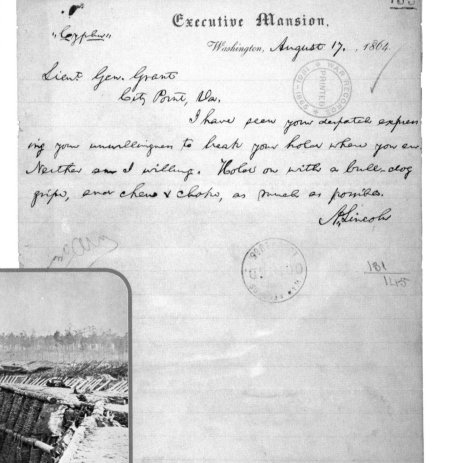

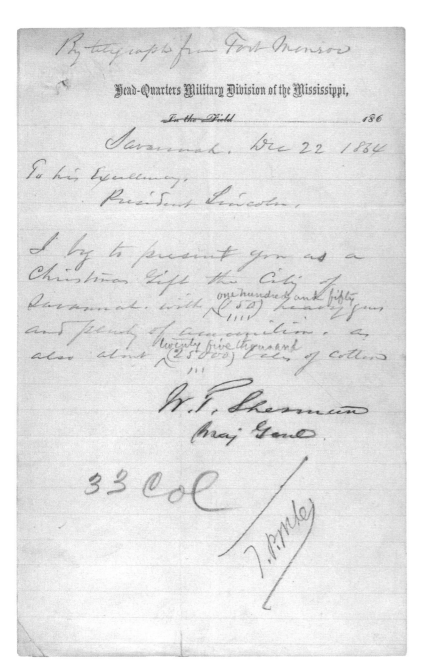

To Maj. Gen. William Tecumseh Sherman, commander of the Union Army's Military Division of the Mississippi, the Civil War was a fight for the survival of the United States as a nation. To win, he believed that he had to wage war not just against the Confederate soldiers but against the people and the economy that sustained them.

In the fall of 1864, General Sherman led his "March to the Sea," one of the most bitterly remembered events of the war. Cutting a 300-mile path of destruction from Atlanta to Savannah, Sherman's men laid waste to 12 percent of Georgia's territory, wreaking havoc on the lives of thousands of citizens and advertising to thousands more the terror that continued resistance would bring. While Sherman's orders prohibited the destruction of private houses and property with no military value, a mob spirit infected the campaign, causing unchecked looting and arson. After reaching Savannah, Sherman estimated that of the $100 million worth of damage resulting from the campaign, 20 percent was for military advantage; the rest, he said, was "simple waste and destruction."

Sherman believed that the people who supported secession were criminals and deserved the terrible consequences that the war had brought to them. Leaving smoldering ruins and bitter memories in his wake, Sherman remained unapologetic: "If the people raise a howl against my barbarity and cruelty, I will answer that war is war and not popularity-seeking."

Telegram from Maj. Gen. William Tecumseh Sherman to President Abraham Lincoln, presenting the city of Savannah as a Christmas gift, December 22, 1864

The culmination of Sherman's "March to the Sea" was the capture of Savannah. With savage irony, Sherman invoked the spirit of Christmas as he informed his Commander-in-Chief that Savannah was taken, complete with 150 heavy guns, plenty of ammunition, and 25,000 bales of cotton.

President Lincoln was thrilled to hear this news, which he immediately publicized throughout the nation.

RECORD GROUP 107, RECORDS OF THE OFFICE OF THE SECRETARY OF WAR

> *I beg to present you as a Christmas gift the City of Savannah.*
>
> MAJ. GEN. WILLIAM TECUMSEH SHERMAN, AT THE END OF THE "MARCH TO THE SEA," TO PRESIDENT ABRAHAM LINCOLN, DECEMBER 22, 1864

> *I know I am in danger; but I am not going to worry over threats like these.*
>
> PRESIDENT ABRAHAM LINCOLN, ON FILING AWAY HIS
> LATEST DEATH THREAT, MARCH 1865

By late March 1865, President Lincoln had grown used to hate mail, threats, and warnings. While he outwardly refused to attach any importance to them, they had begun to haunt his inner life. In a particularly disturbing dream he had in early April, he saw himself wandering from room to room in the White House, following the mysterious sound of people weeping until he arrived in the East Room where he saw a "sickening surprise": the body of the President laid out, the victim of an assassin.

On April 14, 1865, in a chilling fulfillment of this vision, President Lincoln was shot in the back of the head at point blank range while watching a comedy

at Ford's Theatre. He died the following morning at 7:22 a.m. On Wednesday, April 19, thousands of weeping people paid their final respects to the President, filing past his body in the East Room of the White House.

**Police blotter listing the assassination of President Abraham Lincoln,
11 p.m., April 14, 1865**

Detail opposite

The shattering news of the first Presidential assassination in U.S. history appears among the more routine business of the D.C. police: the investigation of a suspicious character, the arrest of a 35-year-old prostitute, and the receipt of a saddle cover, halter, and three fishing lines.

This log shows that the Detective Corps of the District of Columbia Metropolitan Police received news of the assassi-

nation at 11 p.m. "J. Wilks Booth" (John Wilkes Booth) is listed as the assassin. The pages that follow list the witnesses and items that were recovered at the scene. The entry for President Lincoln's assassination begins near the bottom of the page on the right.

RECORD GROUP 351, RECORDS OF THE GOVERNMENT OF THE DISTRICT OF COLUMBIA

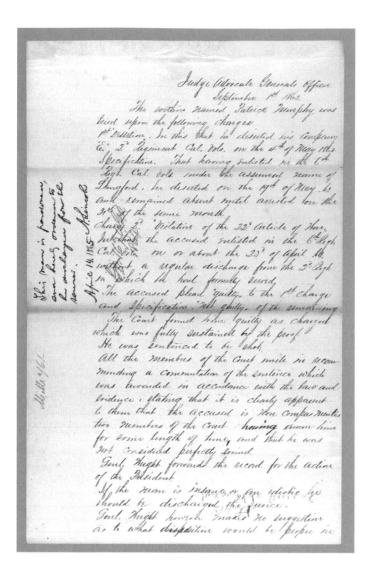

President Abraham Lincoln's pardon of Pvt. Patrick Murphy, April 14, 1865

Lincoln spent most of the last day of his life at work in the White House. He received visitors, held a cabinet meeting, and tended to some paperwork, including the review of a handful of court-martial cases. As President, Lincoln reviewed hundreds of the 80,000 cases tried during the Civil War—those that had been appealed and those involving the death penalty. One of the cases he reviewed that afternoon was that of Pvt. Patrick Murphy who had been sentenced to be shot for desertion.

Murphy was described in this summary of his case as "Insane or idiotic, non compos mentis." Lincoln unceremoniously wrote his decision to pardon Murphy in the corner margin of this page; it was one of the President's last administrative acts.

Lincoln presided over the nation's most terrible crisis. The Civil War began 1 month after he took office and ended 5 days before he died. It was more bitter and protracted than anyone had predicted, costing more than 600,000 lives. In Lincoln's second inaugural address, delivered just over a month before his death, he spoke about the war as he had come to understand it. The unspeakable savagery that had already lasted 4 years, he believed, was nothing short of God's own punishment for the sins of human slavery. And with the war not quite over, he offered this terrible pronouncement:

Fondly do we hope—fervently do we pray—that this mighty scourge of war may speedily pass away. Yet, if God wills that it continue, until all the wealth piled by the bond-men's two hundred and fifty years of unrequited toil shall be sunk, and until every drop of blood drawn with the lash, shall be paid by another drawn by the sword, as was said three thousand years ago, so still it must be said "the judgments of the Lord, are true and righteous altogether."

Finally, in the speech's closing, with these immortal words of reconciliation and healing, he set the tone for his plan for the nation's Reconstruction.

With malice toward none; with charity for all; with firmness in the right, as God gives us to see the right, let us strive on to finish the work we are in; to bind up the nation's wounds; to care for him who shall have borne the battle, and for his widow, and his orphan—to do all which may achieve and cherish a just, and a lasting peace, among ourselves, and with all nations.

Opposite page:

Abraham Lincoln, ca. 1860–65

Photograph from the Mathew Brady Collection

By the 1850s the Underground Railroad had become an elaborate, secret network of escape routes for slaves seeking freedom in the Northern states and Canada. Harriet Tubman, who escaped from slavery herself in 1849, became one of the Railroad's most active and courageous conductors.

After securing her own freedom, Tubman returned to slave territory 19 times, risking her liberty and life, to lead some 300 fugitive slaves to freedom. By the late 1850s, she had settled in Auburn, New York, where she purchased a house from Senator William H. Seward. While a cloak of secrecy obscures to this day the identity of many fugitive slaves who escaped via the Underground Railroad and those who helped them, Harriet Tubman remains known as the "Moses of her people."

Harriet Tubman, not dated
Photograph by H.B. Lindsley
COURTESY OF THE LIBRARY OF CONGRESS, PRINTS AND
PHOTOGRAPHS DIVISION, WASHINGTON, DC

[*Excepting John Brown . . . I know of no one who has willingly encountered more perils and hardships to serve our enslaved people than you have.*

FREDERICK DOUGLASS TO HARRIET TUBMAN, AUGUST 29, 1868

General Affidavit of Harriet Tubman Davis supporting a pension claim for her service during the Civil War, not dated

Tubman's experience in covert activity with the Underground Railroad made her an effective spy. During the Civil War, she served in the Union Army as spy and scout, passing behind Confederate lines, obtaining valuable information.

As the widow of a Civil War veteran, she had been granted a pension of $8 a month in 1890. In this affidavit, she asked for a lump sum of $1800 based on her own service, described here as "nurse and cook in hospitals, and as commander of Several Men (eight or nine) as scouts during the late War of the Rebellion." Unable to read or write, she signed this affidavit with an "X." Although Tubman did not receive the lump sum of $1800 she requested, her pension was increased from $8 to $25 a month in 1899.

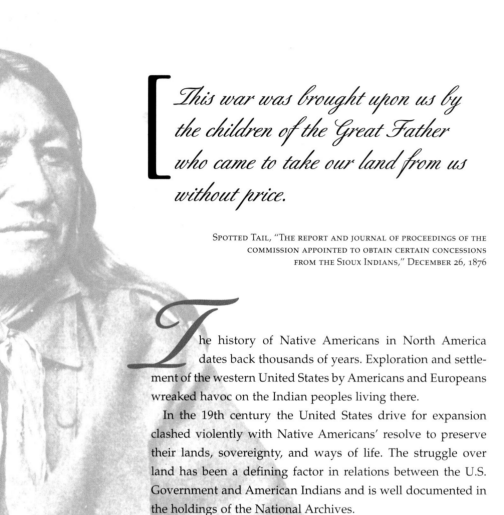

[*This war was brought upon us by the children of the Great Father who came to take our land from us without price.*

SPOTTED TAIL, "THE REPORT AND JOURNAL OF PROCEEDINGS OF THE COMMISSION APPOINTED TO OBTAIN CERTAIN CONCESSIONS FROM THE SIOUX INDIANS," DECEMBER 26, 1876

*T*he history of Native Americans in North America dates back thousands of years. Exploration and settlement of the western United States by Americans and Europeans wreaked havoc on the Indian peoples living there.

In the 19th century the United States drive for expansion clashed violently with Native Americans' resolve to preserve their lands, sovereignty, and ways of life. The struggle over land has been a defining factor in relations between the U.S. Government and American Indians and is well documented in the holdings of the National Archives.

🐚 *Until 1871 the U.S. Government negotiated treaties with Indian tribes as it did with foreign powers. Many of the treaties extinguished Native Americans' title to land. Other agreements related to the pursuit and maintenance of peace, the status of tribes as dependent nations, and regulation of trade. Many of the treaties are still significant in the defense of Indian land claims, hunting and fishing rights, and tribal autonomy.*

"Spotted Tail, a Brulé Sioux chief of great renown"

RECORD GROUP 111, RECORDS OF THE OFFICE OF THE CHIEF SIGNAL OFFICER (111-SC-82538)

Treaty of 1868, April 29, 1868

Page 1 and second signature page

The Black Hills of Dakota are sacred to the Sioux Indians. In the 1868 treaty, signed at Fort Laramie and other military posts in Sioux country, the United States recognized the Black Hills as part of the Great Sioux Reservation, set aside for exclusive use by the Sioux people. However, after the discovery of gold there in 1874, the United States confiscated the land in 1877. To this day, ownership of the Black Hills remains the subject of a legal dispute between the U.S. Government and the Sioux.

The final pages of the 1868 treaty bear the names and markings of the Sioux chiefs and the signatures of the American commissioners who represented the United States.

RECORD GROUP 11, GENERAL RECORDS OF THE U.S. GOVERNMENT

> *Alaska is utterly worthless, and even if it were otherwise, we have no earthly use for it.*

Representative Dennis McCarthy, New York, 1867

"Hello, National Archives?"
Cartoon by Jim Borgman, **Cincinnati Enquirer, ©1993**

In 1993, when Russian nationalist Vladimir Zhirinovsky announced that Russia should take Alaska back, he inspired this editorial cartoon.

Reprinted with special permission King Features Syndicate

In 1866 the Russian government offered to sell the territory of Alaska to the United States. Secretary of State William H. Seward, enthusiastic about the prospect of American expansion, negotiated the deal for the Americans. Edouard de Stoeckl, Russian minister to the United States, negotiated for the Russians. On March 30, 1867, the two parties agreed that the United States would pay Russia $7.2 million for the territory of Alaska.

For less than 2 cents an acre, the United States acquired nearly 600,000 square miles. Opponents of the Alaska Purchase persisted in calling it "Seward's Folly" or "Seward's Icebox" until 1896, when the great Klondike Gold Strike convinced even the harshest critics that Alaska was a valuable addition to American territory.

The undersigned, Envoy Extraordinary and Minister Plenipotentiary
of His Majesty the Emperor of all
the Russias, do hereby acknowledge
to have received at the Treasury Department in Washington Seven
Million Twohundred thousand dollars ($.7.200.000.) in coin, being the
full amount due from The United
States to Russia in consideration
of the cession, by the latter Power
to the former, of certain territory
described in the Treaty entered
into by the Emperor of all the Russias
and the President of the United States
on the 30th day of March 1867.
Washington, August 1st 1868.

Receipt of payment for the purchase of Alaska, August 1, 1868

The receipt states that Edouard de Stoeckl accepted the full payment of $7.2 million at the U.S. Treasury Department in Washington, DC, on behalf of the Emperor of Russia.

RECORD GROUP 217, RECORDS OF THE ACCOUNTING OFFICERS OF THE DEPARTMENT OF THE TREASURY

Cancelled check in the amount of $7.2 million, for the purchase of Alaska, issued August 1, 1868

The check was made payable to the Russian Minister to the United States Edouard de Stoeckl, who negotiated the deal for the Russians.

RECORD GROUP 217, RECORDS OF THE ACCOUNTING OFFICERS OF THE DEPARTMENT OF THE TREASURY

Indictment of Susan B. Anthony for illegal voting, January 24, 1873

Thirteen days after Susan B. Anthony voted in the 1872 election, a deputy U.S. marshal showed up at her house to arrest her.

Two months later, she was indicted for voting illegally on November 5, 1872, "being then and there a person of the female sex." In June she was convicted and sentenced to pay a fine of $100 and court costs.

RECORD GROUP 21, RECORDS OF DISTRICT COURTS OF THE UNITED STATES, NATIONAL ARCHIVES AND RECORDS ADMINISTRATION–NORTHEAST REGION (NEW YORK CITY)

At the time of the first Presidential election in 1789, 6 percent of the population—white, male, property owners—was eligible to vote. The expansion of suffrage—the lifting of restrictions based on religion, race, sex, property ownership, and literacy—has been a gradual process in which many citizens risked their reputations, their jobs, their safety, and sometimes their lives.

Susan B. Anthony championed the causes of antislavery, temperance, and education reform, but she is most closely associated with the fight for woman suffrage to which she devoted herself for 50 years. To test the laws against women voting, she cast ballots for members of Congress and for President in the 1872 election in her hometown of Rochester, New York. For this act she was arrested, tried, and convicted. Anthony died in 1906, 14 years before women gained the vote with the passage of the 19th Amendment to the Constitution.

> *It was we, the people, not we, the white male citizens, nor yet we, the male citizens; but we, the whole people, who formed this Union.*

SUSAN B. ANTHONY, 1873, COMMENTING ON THE PREAMBLE TO THE CONSTITUTION
IN DEFENSE OF WOMEN'S RIGHT TO VOTE

Susan B. Anthony, not dated

RECORD GROUP 86, RECORDS OF THE WOMEN'S BUREAU (86-G-9F-5)

> *Genius is hard work,*
> *stick-to-it-iveness, and*
> *common sense.*
>
> THOMAS A. EDISON

Thomas Edison propelled the United States out of the gaslight era and into the electric age. From the time he was a boy, he was mesmerized by the mechanics of the universe and, with virtually no formal education, brought forth innovations that continue to dominate our lives. Out of his New Jersey laboratories, which were themselves inventions—thoroughly equipped and fully staffed—came 1,093 patented inventions and innovations that made Edison one of the most prolific inventors of all time. Three of his most famous inventions, the phonograph, a practical incandescent light bulb, and the moving picture camera, dazzled the public and revolutionized the way people live throughout the world. His thundering dynamos transformed the United States into the world's greatest industrial superpower.

In 1878, the creation of a practical long-burning electric light had eluded scientists for decades. With dreams of lighting up entire cities, Edison lined up financial backing, assembled a group of brilliant scientists and technicians, and applied his genius to the challenge of creating an effective and affordable electric lamp. With unflagging determination, Edison and his team tried out thousands of theories, convinced that every failure brought them one step closer to success. On January 27, 1880, Edison received the historic patent embodying the principles of his incandescent lamp that paved the way for the universal domestic use of electric light.

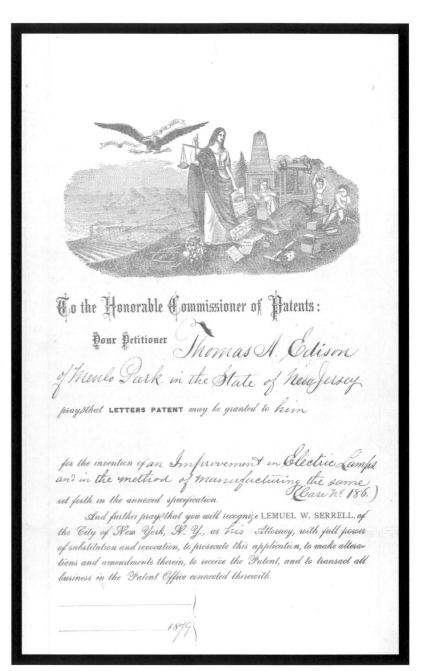

Thomas Edison's patent application for an "Improvement in Electric Lamps," November 1, 1879

RECORD GROUP 241, RECORDS OF THE PATENT AND TRADEMARK OFFICE

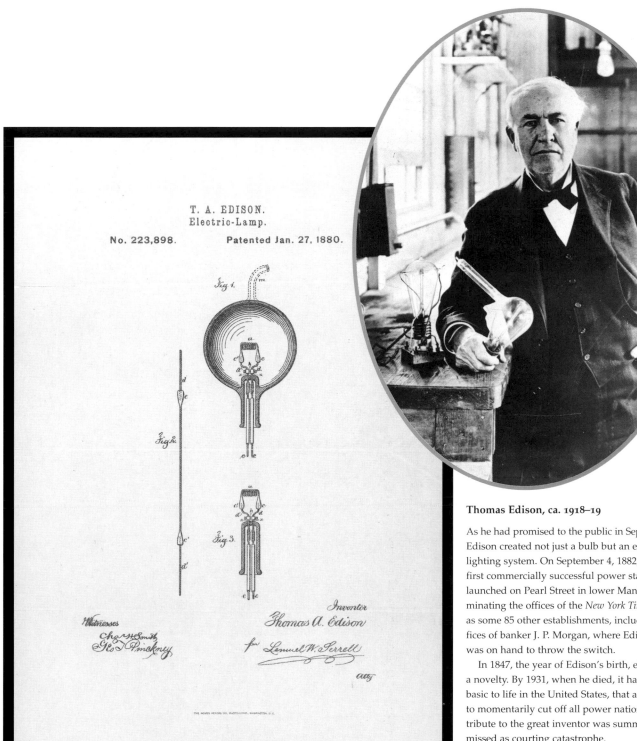

T. A. EDISON.
Electric-Lamp.

No. 223,898.   Patented Jan. 27, 1880.

Thomas Edison's patent drawing for an improvement in electric lamps, patented January 27, 1880

The simple elegance of Edison's design is remarkably similar to the electric bulbs used today.

Thomas Edison, ca. 1918–19

As he had promised to the public in September 1878, Edison created not just a bulb but an entire electric lighting system. On September 4, 1882, the world's first commercially successful power station was launched on Pearl Street in lower Manhattan, illuminating the offices of the *New York Times*, as well as some 85 other establishments, including the offices of banker J. P. Morgan, where Edison himself was on hand to throw the switch.

In 1847, the year of Edison's birth, electricity was a novelty. By 1931, when he died, it had become so basic to life in the United States, that a suggestion to momentarily cut off all power nationwide as a tribute to the great inventor was summarily dismissed as courting catastrophe.

> *"Keep, ancient lands, your storied pomp!" cries she*
> *With silent lips. "Give me your tired, your poor,*
> *Your huddled masses yearning to breathe free,*
> *The wretched refuse of your teeming shore.*
> *Send these, the homeless, tempest-tost to me,*
> *I lift my lamp beside the golden door!"*
>
> FROM "THE NEW COLOSSUS," SONNET BY EMMA LAZARUS,
> INSCRIBED ON THE BASE OF THE STATUE OF LIBERTY

On July 4, 1884, with "Lady Liberty" herself towering over the proceedings in a Paris foundry yard, the people of France formally presented the Statue of Liberty to the people of the United States. The ceremony was a milestone in a project that was the brainchild of a small group of Frenchmen inspired by the American ideal of liberty. Initially conceived as a gift to celebrate the centennial anniversary of the great alliance between France and the United States and its role in securing American independence, the Statue of Liberty has become one of the most poignant and potent symbols of human freedom.

The Statue of Liberty was designed by the French sculptor Frédéric Auguste Bartholdi, who remained passionately devoted to the project from its conception through its dedication. It is a masterpiece of artistic expression and structural engineering. Broken chains of oppression lie at the feet of the goddess of liberty, draped in flowing robes. In one hand she holds a torch of enlightenment and in the other a tablet of law inscribed with the date of American independence. The model for the face of the figure is believed to be the sculptor's mother. The statue is made of 452 copper sheets of $3/32$" thickness, hammered together and fastened to a skeletal structure that was designed and constructed by Alexandre Gustave Eiffel, the French engineer who later designed the Eiffel Tower.

One of the colossal sculptures of the world, the statue has greeted millions of travelers and immigrants arriving in New York harbor throughout the 20th century. The famous sonnet by Emma Lazarus, inscribed on the pedestal, gives voice to a strain of idealism that celebrates the United States as a haven for the oppressed peoples of the world:

> *Not like the brazen giant of Greek fame,*
> *With conquering limbs astride from land to land;*
> *Here at our sea-washed, sunset gates shall stand*
> *A mighty woman with a torch, whose flame*
> *Is the Imprisoned lightning, and her name*
> *Mother of Exiles. From her beacon-hand*
> *Glows world-wide welcome; her mild eyes command*
> *The air-bridged harbor that twin cities frame.*
> *"Keep, ancient lands, your storied pomp!" cries she*
> *With silent lips. "Give me your tired, your poor,*
> *Your huddled masses yearning to breathe free,*
> *The wretched refuse of your teeming shore.*
> *Send these, the homeless, tempest-tost to me,*
> *I lift my lamp beside the golden door!"*

Official Presentation of "Liberty Enlightening the World," Paris, July 4, 1884
Printed in *Frank Leslie's Illustrated Newspaper*, June 13, 1885
COURTESY OF THE LIBRARY OF CONGRESS, PRINTS AND PHOTOGRAPHS DIVISION, WASHINGTON, DC

Deed of Gift, Statue of Liberty, July 4, 1884

With this document, the people of France present and
the people of the United States accept the sculpture,
"Liberty Enlightening the World." For nearly 3 years,
the assembly of the statue in the courtyard of the
French construction firm Gaget, Gauthier, et Cie
created a spectacular outdoor attraction as the statue
grew from the bottom up. Completed in the spring of
1884, the statue towered over the streets of Paris,
dwarfing everything in sight, until January 1885, when
it was dismantled, packed in 214 crates, and shipped to
the United States for its final installation in New York
harbor. The statue was dedicated on Bedloe's Island
(later renamed Liberty Island) on October 28, 1886.

Record Group 59, General Records of the Department of State

*To the time-honored friendship
of France and the United States*

*The fourth of July, the year one thousand
eight hundred eighty-four, anniversary day
of the Independence of the United States. In
the presence of Monsieur Jules Ferry, President of the Council of Ministers, Minister of
Foreign Affairs, Monsieur Ferdinand de
Lesseps, in the name of the Committee of the
Franco-American Union and of the national
demonstration of which the Committee is the
voice, presented the colossal statue of "Liberty
Enlightening the World," work of sculptor
A. Bartholdi, to his Excellency Monsieur
Morton Minister Plenipotentiary of the
United States in Paris in requesting him to
be the bearer of the sentiments of which this
work is the expression. Monsieur Morton, in
the name of his fellow countrymen, thanks
the Franco-American Union for this evidence
of goodwill of the French people; he proclaims
that in virtue of the powers conferred upon
him by the President of the United States
and the Committee for the work in America
represented by its honorable President Mr.
William M. Evarts, he accepts the statue and
that it will be erected by the American people, conforming to the vote of Congress of 22
February 1877, in the harbor of New-York in
remembrance of the time-honored friendship
that unites the two nations.*

In faith of which have signed:

*In the name of France,
Jules Brisson, President of the Chamber
Jules Ferry, Minister of Foreign Affairs*

*In the name of the United States,
Levi P. Morton, Minister of the United States*

*In the name of the Committee of the Franco-
 American Union,
Ferdinand De Lesseps
E. De Lafayette*

> *Who wouldn't be a mountaineer!*
> *I feel like preaching these mountains*
> *like an apostle.*

JOHN MUIR, *My First Summer in the Sierra*, 1911

To the Chairman of the
Committee on Agriculture
House of Representatives
Washington , D.C.

Dear Sir,
Whereas at a meeting of the Sierra Club of Saturday, November 5th 1892, said club being a corporation formed for the purposes, to wit : "To explore, enjoy and render accessible the mou...Coast ; to publish authentic... to enlist the support and co-...the government in preserving features of the Sierra Nevada was introduced and unani... the Board of Directors to pre... against Bill H.R 5764 in and to use every effort to de... Therefore The ...Club in accordance with the and emphatically protest a...the Yosemite National Park contemplated in Bill H.R. Caminetti and referred by th...your honorable Committee...As shown in a...

tributaries of the Tuolumne River as it passes through the Grand Cañon of the Tuolumne River finally through Hetch-Hetchy Valley , a valley which in grandeur & uniqueness is in many respects the peer of Yosemite and will in future form one of the principal attractions of the Sierra Nevada of California

If the territory of the Yosemite National Park should be reduced in accordance with the bill H.R 5764, the dangers to guard against which the Park was originally set aside , would again arise , the herds of sheep which now for two seasons have successfully been kept out of the preservation would denude the watersheds of their vegetation , the forest fires following in the wake of the herds would destroy the magnificent forests and threaten the reservation itself and the timber of priceless value to the prosperity of the State would become the prey of the speculator.

The Directors of the Sierra Club respectfully point out that Senate Bill No 3235 proposed by Mr. Paddock will meet any objections in the interest of mining or farming industries if there be any, to the continuance of the present limits of the Yosemite National Park Reservation.

John Muir
President Sierra Club
J. H. Senger,
Secretary Sierra Club
Warren Olney
First Vice-President Sierra Club.
San Francisco, Jan 2nd 1893

Sierra Club petition protesting the reduction of Yosemite National Park, January 2, 1893
Page 1 and signature page

The Yosemite Act of 1890 established Yosemite National Park in California. Throughout the 1890s speculators and developers agitated to reduce the size of the park. This petition, signed by John Muir and other members of the Sierra Club, protests one of these efforts. The bill referred to in the petition was defeated.

John Muir's life was driven by the joys he found in nature. With an almost religious fervor, he preached the glories of the American wilderness, which he experienced firsthand in California's Sierra Nevada Range and in the Yosemite Valley.

In the early 1890s Muir became one of the nation's most effective messengers for the cause of wilderness preservation. He believed that the best hope to protect the wilderness lay in the U.S. Government, which had established Yellowstone National Park, the world's first national park, in 1872. Muir was a founding member and president of the Sierra Club, which is still one of the leading conservation organizations in the nation.

OPPOSITE PAGE:

"Yosemite National Park, Calif. Cathedral Spires in Yosemite Valley," 1892
Photograph by John K. Hillers

> [*Oh, honest Americans, as Christians hear me for my down-trodden people. Their form of government is as dear to them as yours is precious to you.*

QUEEN LILIUOKALANI, LAST REIGNING MONARCH OF HAWAII, 1898

In the 1890s the efforts of the Hawaiian people to preserve their national sovereignty and native heritage ran headlong into the unstoppable force of American expansionism. Throughout the 19th century, westerners—particularly Americans—came to dominate Hawaii's economy and politics. When Queen Liliuokalani assumed the throne in 1891 and tried to reassert the power of the throne and the will of the Native Hawaiians, she was deposed by a small group of American businessmen, with the support of American diplomats and the U.S. Navy.

Although even President Cleveland challenged the legitimacy of this takeover, it did stand. To a nation poised to take its place as a world power, the control of Hawaii, strategically located to serve as a mid-Pacific naval installation, seemed crucial. In 1898, with a naval base firmly established at Pearl Harbor, the United States officially annexed Hawaii.

Letter from Liliuokalani to the U.S. House of Representatives protesting the American takeover of the Hawaiian Islands, December 19, 1898

Liliuokalani placed great hope and faith in the United States. Even after Hawaiian annexation, she and others representing the Native Hawaiians tried to hold the United States to its own highest ideals of political self-determination, citing the very principles expressed in the Declaration of Independence.

One hundred years after the Queen was forced from her throne, the United States formally apologized to Native Hawaiians for the illegal overthrow of the Kingdom of Hawaii.

RECORD GROUP 233, RECORDS OF THE U.S. HOUSE OF REPRESENTATIVES, REPRODUCED WITH THE PERMISSION OF THE U.S. HOUSE OF REPRESENTATIVES

Her Majesty Queen Liliuokalani, 1891–92

Though well schooled in western culture, Liliuokalani was descended from generations of chiefs and was adored by the people of Hawaii. (She was also an accomplished musician whose best-known composition is "Aloha Oe, Farewell to Thee.") After being forced from her throne, she traveled to the United States, where she participated in a massive lobbying effort to restore the Hawaiian lands to the Hawaiian people. Despite a campaign that swayed several members of Congress, Hawaii became an American territory on August 12, 1898.

COURTESY OF THE BISHOP MUSEUM, HONOLULU, HAWAII

Federal meat inspectors examining beef carcasses, ca. 1910–20

RECORD GROUP 16, RECORDS OF THE OFFICE OF THE SECRETARY OF AGRICULTURE (16-G-239-2499-C)

"Muckraker" is the term Theodore Roosevelt used to label writers and journalists of the early 1900s who wrote to expose and, ultimately, reform the ills and corruptions that plagued many of the nation's public and private institutions. In *The Jungle*, author Upton Sinclair took aim at the brutalization and exploitation of workingmen in a Chicago meat-packing house; however, it was the filthy conditions, described in nauseating detail—and the threat they posed to meat consumers—that caused a public furor.

Public reaction to the book was a major factor in the passage of the 1907 Meat Inspection Act, which established a system of meat inspection that endured for nearly a century. In July 1996, the Federal Government announced new rules requiring more scientifically advanced methods of meat inspection.

I aimed at the public's heart and by accident hit it in the stomach.

UPTON SINCLAIR, ON THE PUBLIC REACTION TO HIS BOOK *The Jungle*

Letter from Upton Sinclair to President Theodore Roosevelt, March 10, 1906

Page 1 and signature page

In this letter to President Roosevelt, Sinclair supported the presence of Federal inspectors in the meat-packing houses, but he advised that inspectors should come disguised as working-men to discover the true conditions, as Sinclair did when he researched his book.

RECORD GROUP 16, RECORDS OF THE OFFICE OF THE SECRETARY OF AGRICULTURE

"The Jungle," a Story of Packingtown.

The "Uncle Tom's Cabin" of wage slavery.—JACK LONDON.

The greatest novel written in America in fifty years.—DAVID GRAHAM PHILLIPS

The Jungle Publishing Co.

Publishers of the books of Upton Sinclair.

P. O. Box 2064, New York City.

(Letters intended for Upton Sinclair personally should be addressed to Princeton, N. J.)

King Midas: A Romance.
The Journal of Arthur Stirling.
Prince Hagen: A Phantasy.
Manassas: A Novel of the War.

March 10, 1906.

President Theodore Roosevelt,
Washington, D. C.

My dear President Roosevelt:

I have just returned from some ex-
ploring in the Jersey glass factories and find your kind note.
I am glad to learn that the Department of Agriculture has taken
up the matter of inspection, or lack of it, but I am exceedingly
dubious as to what they will discover. I have seen so many people go out there and be put off with smooth pretences. A man has
to be something of a
men, as I was, before
is becoming a great d
"The Jungle." I hav
of Armour & Company,
Ray Stannard Baker ir
and a half ago. He r
'the lid is on' in Pa
places where before l
that the thing which
is a matter of hundre
in to-day's "Saturday
article (which I hap
mer) that "In Armour

\-\-7\-\-

You ask - "Is there anything further, say in the Department of Agriculture, which you would suggest my doing?" I would
suggest the following: That you do as Doubleday, Page & Company
did; find a man concerning whose intelligence and integrity you
are absolutely sure; send him up here, or let me meet him in
Washington, and tell him all that I saw, and how I saw it, and
give him the names and addresses of the people who will enable
him to see it. Then let him go to Packingtown as I did, as a working-man; live with the men, get a job in the yards, and use his
eyes and ears; and see if he does not come out at the end of a few
weeks feeling, as did the special correspondent of the London
"Lancet," whom I met in Chicago, that the conditions in the packing-houses constitute a "menace to the health of the civilized
world." *The Lancet for Jan 8, 15, 22, 29 — 1905.*

Thanking you for your kind interest,

Very sincerely,

Upton Sinclair

P. S.

I might add that when I was in Chicago I learned a good
deal about the connections which the packers have in Washington,
so that I think it most likely that before the Department of
Agriculture got anybody started for the purpose of investigating
Packingtown, word had been sent there to the packing-houses that
things should be cleaned up. I know positively that this was done
in the case of Major Seaman, who went out there for "Collier's
Weekly."

EXCERPTS OF THE LETTER FROM PAGES 3–4 AND 6–7

I saw with my own eyes hams, which had spoiled in pickle, being pumped full of chemicals to destroy the odor. I saw waste ends of smoked beef stored in barrels in a cellar, in a condition of filth which I could not describe in a letter. I saw rooms in which sausage meat was stored, with poisoned rats lying about, and the dung of rats covering them. I saw hogs which had died of cholera in shipment, being loaded into box cars to be taken to a place called Globe, in Indiana, to be rendered into lard. . . .

This is a very long letter, but I feel the importance of the subject excuses it. It would give me great pleasure to come down to Washington to see you at any time, but I would rather it was after you had read "The Jungle," because I have put a good deal of myself into that.

You ask—"Is there anything further, say in the Department of Agriculture, which you would suggest my doing?" I would suggest the following: That you do as Doubleday, Page & Company did; find a man concerning whose intelligence and integrity you are absolutely sure; send him up here, or let me meet him in Washington, and tell him all that I saw, and how I saw it, and give him the names and addresses of the people who will enable him to see it. Then let him go to Packingtown as I did, as a working-man; live with the men, get a job in the yards, and use his eyes and ears; and see if he does not come out at the end of a few weeks feeling, as did the special correspondent of the London "Lancet," whom I met in Chicago, that the conditions in the packing-houses constitute a "menace to the health of the civilized world."

> *Not even God himself could sink this ship.*
>
> EMPLOYEE OF THE WHITE STAR LINE, AT THE LAUNCH OF THE *Titanic*, MAY 31, 1911

When the British ship *Titanic* steamed out of Southampton bound for New York on April 10, 1912, it was the largest and most sumptuous luxury liner that had ever sailed. It was a monument to the promise of technology and to Victorian elegance, magnificently appointed with oriental carpets and crystal chandeliers. It was thought to be unsinkable.

Confidence was so high that the owners and builders rejected plans calling for as many as 64 lifeboats. Although the number of lifeboats on the *Titanic* (20) exceeded Government standards, the boats would only accommodate about half of the 2,228 people aboard. In one of history's great ironies, the *Titanic* sank on its maiden voyage, after colliding with an iceberg off the banks of Newfoundland. More than 1,500 people died in the accident.

Records relating to the *Titanic* are from a case file of a limitation of liability suit brought by the ship's owners 3 years after it sank.

Lifeboat filled with survivors of the *Titanic* waiting to be rescued, April 15, 1912

This photograph was taken by a passenger of the *Carpathia,* the ship that received the *Titanic's* distress signal and came to rescue the survivors.

RECORD GROUP 21, RECORDS OF DISTRICT COURTS OF THE UNITED STATES, NATIONAL ARCHIVES AND RECORDS ADMINISTRATION–NORTHEAST REGION (NEW YORK CITY)

OPPOSITE PAGE:

U.S. Navy daily memorandum reporting the *Titanic's* collision with an iceberg, April 15, 1912

RECORD GROUP 21, RECORDS OF DISTRICT COURTS OF THE UNITED STATES, NATIONAL ARCHIVES AND RECORDS ADMINISTRATION–NORTHEAST REGION (NEW YORK CITY)

HYDROGRAPHIC OFFICE,
WASHINGTON, D. C.

DAILY MEMORANDUM

N-8.

No. 1013.   April 15, 1912.

N O R T H   A T L A N T I C   O C E A N

OBSTRUCTIONS OFF THE AMERICAN COAST.

Mar. 28 - Lat 24° 20', lon 80° 02', passed a broken spar projecting about 3 feet out of water, apparently attached to sunken wreckage.--EVELYN (SS) Wright.

OBSTRUCTIONS ALONG THE OVER-SEA ROUTES.

Apr 7 - Lat 35° 20', lon 59° 40', saw a lowermast covered with marine growth.--ADRIATICO (It. ss), Cevascu.

ICE REPORTS.

Apr 7 - Lat 45° 10', lon 56° 40', ran into a strip of field ice about 3 or 4 miles wide extending north and south as far as could be seen. Some very heavy pans were seen.--ROSALIND (Br ss), Williams.

Apr 10 - Lat 41° 50', lon 50 25', passed a large ice field a few hundred feet wide and 15 miles long extending in a NNE direction.--EXCELSION (Ger ss). (New York Herald)

COLLISION WITH ICEBERG - Apr 14 - Lat 41° 46', lon 50° 14', the British steamer TITANIC collided with an iceberg seriously damaging her bow; extent not definitely known.

Apr 14 - The German steamer AMERIKA reported by radio telegraph passing two large icebergs in lat 41° 27', lon 50° 08',--TITANIC (Br ss).

Apr 14 - Lat 42° 06', lon 49° 43', encountered extensive field ice and saw seven icebergs of considerable size.--PISA (Ger ss).

J. J. K N A P P

Captain, U. S. Navy,
Hydrographer.

Villa, dead or alive.

<small>SLOGAN ADOPTED BY U.S. TROOPS CHARGED WITH
THE CAPTURE OF FRANCISCO ("PANCHO") VILLA, 1916</small>

On March 9, 1916, Francisco ("Pancho") Villa, the Mexican Revolutionary general, ordered a charge of some 485 men into the sleepy, sun-baked, desert outpost of Columbus, New Mexico. There they terrorized the town's 350 inhabitants, killed 18 Americans, and set fire to the wooden buildings before retreating back across the Mexican border.

President Woodrow Wilson retaliated by ordering a force of men, that eventually numbered 14,000, under the command of Gen. John J. Pershing, to cross into Mexico and capture Villa. The Mexican Punitive Expedition was a conspicuous display of American might that included the first American use of airplanes in military conflict. But the Mexican terrain was hostile and Villa elusive. Although the Expedition probably deterred similar raids on American settlements, it ended after 11 months with Pancho Villa still at large.

"Gen. Pancho Villa–Taken in Ojinaga–Sunday Jan. 11th 1914"

Villa emerged as a serious contender for power during the Mexican Revolution. He championed the cause of the common man and railed against the threat of foreign, especially American, interests.

<small>RECORD GROUP 111, RECORDS OF THE OFFICE OF THE CHIEF SIGNAL OFFICER (111-SC-82925)</small>

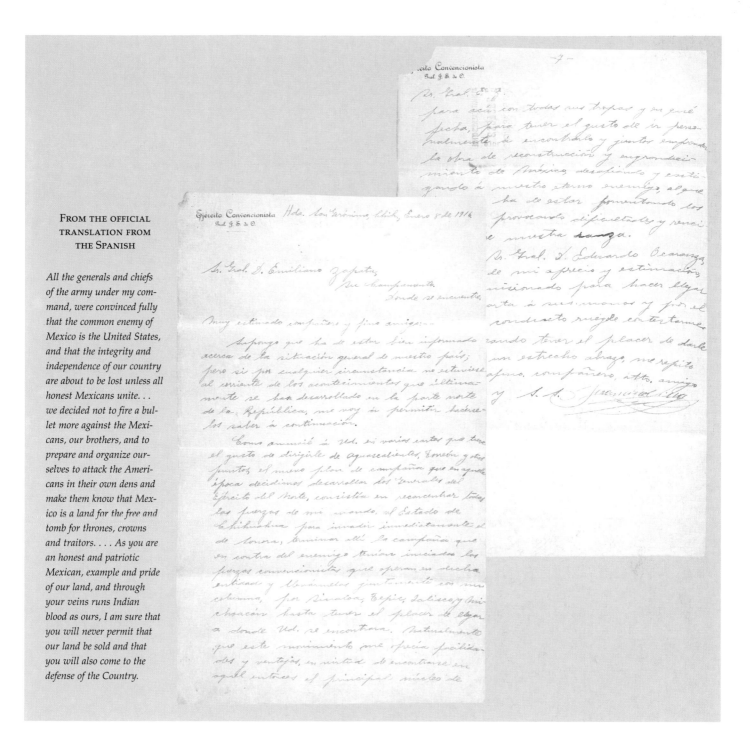

Letter from Gen. Francisco Villa to Gen. Emiliano Zapata, January 8, 1916

Page 1 and signature page

This letter, written and signed by Francisco Villa, was found in the saddlebag of one of his officers killed during the New Mexico raid.

In the letter, Villa proposed that General Zapata, the leading Revolutionary general in southern Mexico, join forces with Villa in the north to launch a campaign against their common enemy, the United States.

Record Group 94, Records of the Adjutant General's Office, 1780's–1917

4458   gemeinsam
17149   Friedenschluß .
14471   ☉
6706   reichlich
13850   finanziell
12224   unterstützung
6929   und
14991   einverständnis
7382   unsererseits .
158(5)7 da/3
67893   Mexico .
14218   in
36477   Texas
5870   ⑤
17553   neu
67893   Mexico .
5870   ③
5454   AR
16102   IZ
15217   ON
22801   A

Decode of the Zimmermann Telegram made by Edward Bell of the American Embassy in London, sent to the Department of State, March 2, 1917

Selected page

Texas, New Mexico, and Arizona, the states that Germany pledged to help Mexico recover, are mentioned in this portion of the decode.

[*We make Mexico a proposal of alliance on the following basis: Make war together, make peace together.*

ZIMMERMANN TELEGRAM, JANUARY 16, 1917

On January 16, 1917, in the midst of the European war that would later be known as World War I, German Foreign Minister Arthur Zimmermann sent an encoded message to be conveyed to the President of Mexico, proposing a military alliance against the United States. In return for Mexican support in the war, Germany would help Mexico regain New Mexico, Texas, and Arizona from the United States. The British intercepted the secret message, deciphered it, and turned it over to the U.S. Government.

Public revelation of the Zimmermann Telegram in the United States on March 1, 1917, came at a crucial moment. By the spring of 1917, German submarine warfare had killed nearly 200 Americans. The United States had recently broken diplomatic relations with Germany in response to the German decision to begin unrestricted submarine warfare. The Zimmermann Telegram further inflamed U.S. public opinion against Germany, particularly in the western and southwestern United States. On April 2, President Woodrow Wilson asked Congress to declare war against Germany and the Central Powers; on April 6, Congress complied.

OPPOSITE PAGE:

Photostat of Zimmermann Telegram, as received by the German Ambassador to Mexico, January 19, 1917

The idea that Germany was proposing to give away a chunk of the United States to Mexico was so outlandish, many people doubted the telegram's authenticity. This copy, obtained by the Department of State from Western Union, and the decode of the message served to authenticate the Zimmermann Telegram.

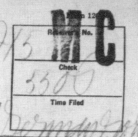

WESTERN UNION TELEGRAM

CLASS OF SERVICE DESIRED

Fast Day Message	X
Day Letter	
Night Message	
Night Letter	

Patrons should mark an X opposite the class of service desired; OTHERWISE THE TELEGRAM WILL BE TRANSMITTED AS A FAST DAY MESSAGE.

NEWCOMB CARLTON, PRESIDENT

Send the following telegram, subject to the terms on back hereof, which are hereby agreed to

via Galveston

JAN 19 1917

GERMAN LEGATION

MEXICO CITY

130	13042	13401	8501	115	3528	416	17214	6491	11310
18147	18222	21560	10247	11518	23677	13605	3494	14936
98092	5905	11311	10392	10371	0302	21290	5161	39695
23571	17504	11269	18276	18101	0317	0228	17694	4473
23284	22200	19452	21589	67893	5569	13918	8958	12137
1333	4725	4458	5905	17166	13851	4458	17149	14471	6706
13850	12224	6929	14991	7382	15857	67893	14218	36477
5870	17553	67893	5870	5454	16102	15217	22801	17138
21001	17388	7446	23638	18222	6719	14331	15021	23845
3156	23552	22096	21604	4797	9497	22464	20855	4377
23610	18140	22260	5905	13347	20420	39689	13732	20667
6929	5275	18507	52262	1340	22049	13339	11265	22295
10439	14814	4178	6992	8784	7632	7357	6926	52262	11267
21100	21272	9346	9559	22464	15874	18502	18500	15857
2188	5376	7381	98092	16127	13486	9350	9220	76036	14219
5144	2831	17920	11347	17142	11264	7667	7762	15099	9110
10482	97556	3569	3670					

BERNSTORFF.

Charge German Embassy.

> *It seems to me that Russia is about to be the stage on which will be acted one of the most terrible tragedies of all history. . . . Russia will fairly swim in blood, a prey to lawlessness and violence.*
>
> ROBERT LANSING, SECRETARY OF STATE, DECEMBER 2–4, 1917

As World War I raged in Europe, the stunning events of the Russian Revolution unfolded in the capital city of Petrograd (St. Petersburg). Although the roots of the Russian Revolution were deep and far-reaching, it was the colossal strain of fighting World War I that forced the complete breakdown of Russia's centuries-old political and social institutions.

In February 1917, the Russian tsarist monarchy collapsed and was replaced by the Provisional Government. Seeing a promise of democratic stability, the United States immediately welcomed the new government into the worldwide community of democratic nations. Nine months later, the Bolshevik Revolution overthrew the Provisional Government, replacing it with the world's first Socialist state in history under the leadership of Vladimir Lenin, Leon Trotsky, and Joseph Stalin. The first weeks of Bolshevik power were characterized by confusion and uncertainty, disorder and violence. The world diplomatic community, including the United States, struggled to formulate a response, as they waited to see whether the Bolsheviks would maintain their hold or be swept away.

Keys to the American Embassy in Petrograd

In a gesture of support to the Russian people, the United States opted to maintain a diplomatic presence in a country even while refusing to recognize its government. As the Germans closed in on Petrograd in February 1918, the U.S. Ambassador moved the Embassy to Vologda, some 300 miles to the east. Ambassador Francis left Russia for the last time in November 1918, and the keys to the American Embassy in Petrograd were later sent to Washington, DC.

RECORD GROUP 59, GENERAL RECORDS OF THE DEPARTMENT OF STATE

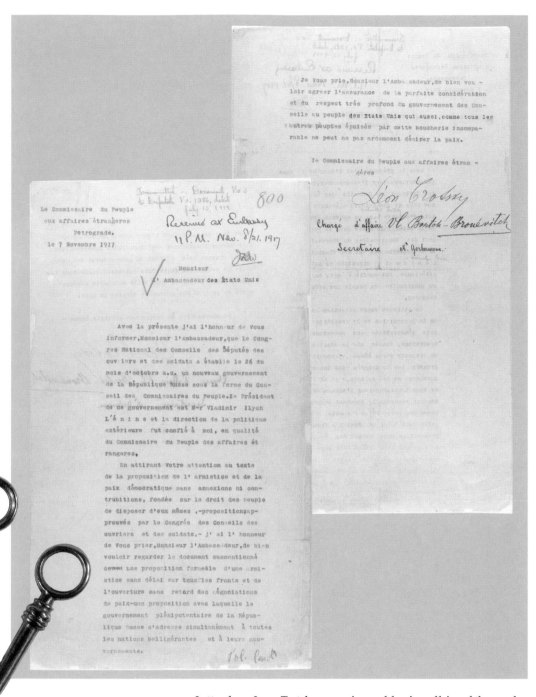

OFFICIAL TRANSLATION
FROM THE FRENCH

THE COMMISSARY OF THE PEOPLE
FOR FOREIGN AFFAIRS, PETROGRAD,
NOVEMBER 7TH, 1917

Mr. Ambassador of the United-States.

By the present I have the honor to inform you, Mr. Ambassador, that the National Congress of the Councils of the Deputies of the Workmen and Soldiers established on the 26th of the month of October of this year [November 8], a new Government of the Russian Republic under the form of the Council of the Commissaries of the People. The president of this Government is Mr. Vladimir Ilyitch Lenine and the management of the foreign policy was intrusted [sic] to me as commissary of the People for Foreign Affairs.

In drawing your attention to the text of the proposition for an armistice and a democratic peace without annexations and contributions founded on the right of people to dispose of themselves, proposals approved by the Congress of the Councils of the Workmen and Soldiers, I have the honor to beg you Mr. Ambassador, to be good enough to regard the above mentioned as a form of proposal for an armistice without delay on all the fronts, and for the opening without delay of negotiations for peace—a proposal which the Plenipotentiary Government of the Russian Republic is addressing simultaneously to all the belligerent nations and to their Governments.

I beg you Mr. Ambassador, to be good enough to accept the assurance of the perfect consideration and profound respect of the Government of the Councils for the people of the United States, who also, like all the other peoples exhausted by this incomparable butchery cannot help but ardently desire peace.

The Commissary of the People for Foreign Affairs:
Signed Leon Trotzky

Chargé d'Affaires:
Brontch Brouevitch

Secretary: Gorbunov

Letter from Leon Trotsky, commissar of foreign affairs of the newly formed Soviet government, to U.S. Ambassador David Francis, received at the Embassy on November 21, 1917

Two weeks after the November Revolution, the U.S. Embassy received the first formal notification of the establishment of a new Soviet regime. This letter also refers to the Soviet Decree on Peace, issued on the first day of Soviet rule, which appealed to the people of all nations to bypass their existing governments in the pursuit of world peace.

On December 1, U.S. Ambassador Francis was instructed to make no reply to this or any other Soviet communication. Viewing the Soviet power as illegitimate—as established by force and not representative of the Russian people—the United States offered no formal recognition of the Soviet Union until 1933.

RECORD GROUP 59, GENERAL RECORDS OF THE DEPARTMENT OF STATE

Note on Dates: The date on this document, November 7, 1917, corresponds to the Julian calendar which was retained by Russia until February 14, 1918. According to the Gregorian calendar, the document would be dated November 20. The dates referred to in these captions correspond to the Gregorian calendar which is 13 days ahead of its Julian counterpart.

"Scene in the Grande Place showing the remains of the Cloth Hall and Cathedral, Ypres, Belgium," not dated

RECORD GROUP 165, RECORDS OF THE WAR DEPARTMENT GENERAL AND SPECIAL STAFFS (165-BO-1188)

*I*n 1917, when the United States entered the European conflict now known as World War I, the nations of Europe were deadlocked in a savage war that was consuming an entire generation of their men. The populations of Europe learned the bitter lessons of modern warfare as the conflict settled into a long, hard war of attrition that killed people—soldiers and civilians—in unprecedented numbers and disrupted the world's political, economic, and social institutions. The United States helped break the stalemate when it joined Britain and France and their allies after a series of provocations by Germany. America's purpose, as expressed by President Wilson, was to "make the world safe for democracy." The Armistice was signed on November 11, 1918.

> *It is hard to find a satisfactory "official" name for the war, but the best, I think, that has been suggested is "The World War."*
>
> PRESIDENT WOODROW WILSON, JULY 31, 1919

OPPOSITE PAGE:

Letter from President Woodrow Wilson to Secretary of War Newton D. Baker, July 31, 1919

On July 23, 1919, the Secretary of War asked the President to "give a name to the war." Among the proposed names were "The Great War," "The World War," "The War of 1917," and "The War Against Teutonic Aggression." Baker stated that his own preference was "The World War."

The war that President Wilson named "The World War" transformed the world. The political map of Europe was rearranged; the United States emerged as a world economic and military power; the Russian Revolution gave birth to the Soviet Union; and the bloodletting in warfare was pushed to new limits, forever blurring the line between military and civilian targets. The harsh terms of the peace settlement set the stage for an even more devastating conflict of World War II.

RECORD GROUP 407, RECORDS OF THE ADJUTANT GENERAL'S OFFICE, 1917–

THE WHITE HOUSE
WASHINGTON

31 July, 1919.

My dear Mr. Secretary:

It is hard to find a satisfactory "official" name for the war, but the best, I think, that has been suggested is "The World War", and I hope that your judgment will concur.

I know you will understand the brevity of this note.

Cordially and faithfully yours,

Woodrow Wilson

Hon. Newton D. Baker,
Secretary of War.

File rec.
10-31-19

*I*n 1882 Helen Keller, a healthy and exceptionally happy and outgoing toddler was robbed of her sight and hearing by a high fever. Cut off from the world she had known, she lived the next 5 years in what she later described as a state of anarchy, sinking deeper and deeper into an angry, uncomprehending, and lonely despair. "Gradually I got used to the silence and darkness that surrounded me and forgot that it had ever been different," Keller wrote, "until she came—my teacher—who was to set my spirit free."

With the assistance of her beloved teacher, Anne Sullivan, Keller went to school and eventually graduated from Radcliffe College. Her astonishing achievements made her a national celebrity by the time she was 20. Throughout her long life, she was a tireless activist for blind and deaf-blind people, traveling the world to convey a message of hope and inspiration. Of all her work—writings, speeches, personal appearances—it is her life itself and the joy she took in it that is the most powerful symbol of triumph over adversity. In 1964 Keller received the nation's highest honor awarded a civilian, the Presidential Medal of Freedom.

OPPOSITE PAGE:

Letter from Helen Keller to President Herbert Hoover, February 5, 1933

In this letter Helen Keller invites President Hoover to join her in a visit to a sound recording studio in New York City where a new technology of talking books was being developed for blind people. Although Keller initially resisted talking books in favor of braille materials, she eventually became convinced of their value and contributed vitally to a publicity campaign. She recalled Hoover's earlier support of blind people and offered the President, who left office in the darkest days of the Great Depression, her own unique brand of inspiration and encouragement. One of Hoover's last acts as President was signing a law dedicating funds from a books-for-the-blind program to the purchase of talking books.

Keller's signature is in her square hand script, which she learned as a young girl using a special writing board to help her stay within the horizontal lines of a page.

NATIONAL ARCHIVES AND RECORDS ADMINISTRATION, HERBERT HOOVER LIBRARY, WEST BRANCH, IOWA

[*She is fellow to Caesar, Alexander, Napoleon, Homer, Shakespeare, and the rest of the immortals.*

MARK TWAIN, ON HELEN KELLER

EXCERPT FROM LETTER

Your presence at the Foundation studio would give a tremendous impetus to this project, and the blind of this country would be gladdened by a message from you saying that a new pathway of light is being blazed through their darkness. It would make me very happy if you should appear with me in a short news reel.

Always I glow with a grateful remembrance of the time when you received the delegates to the World Conference for the Blind. Your fine spirit of cooperation and Mrs. Hoover's gracious hospitality are precious memories in my work. The blind of America will have another reason to remember you with gratitude if you can grant this request. I know how very heavy the burden you are carrying is, and my letter stirs in me an ache of sympathy. But we are told that if we "take His Yoke upon us and learn of Him," we shall find the burden light and the yoke easy.

❦ *Helen Keller was invited to the White House by every President from Grover Cleveland to Lyndon Johnson. Many of the Presidential libraries hold records documenting Keller's encounters with the Presidents.*

7111 SEMINOLE AVENUE
FOREST HILLS, NEW YORK

February 5, 1933

President Herbert Hoover,
The White House,
Washington, D. C.
Dear Mr. President,

You have no doubt been communicated with in regard to the wish of the American Foundation for the Blind that you should visit their sound recording studio while you are in New York on February 13th.

The Foundation is perfec... publishing for the blind, and... pleted, it will supply librar... with talking books recorded o... If this plan succeeds, the bl... ear just as they now listen t... or a speech over the radio.... reading will be brought withi... who, losing their sight late... learning to read with their f...

Your presence at the Fou... a tremendous impetus to this... of this country would be glad... you saying that a new pathway... through their darkness. It w...

7111 SEMINOLE AVENUE
FOREST HILLS, NEW YORK

if you should appear with me in a short news reel.

Always I glow with a grateful remembrance of the time when you received the delegates to the World Conference for the Blind. Your fine spirit of cooperation and Mrs. Hoover's gracious hospitality are precious memories in my work. The blind of America will have another reason to remember you with gratitude if you can grant this request. I know how very heavy the burden you are carrying is, and my letter stirs in me an ache of sympathy. But we are told that if we "take His Yoke upon us and learn of Him," we shall find the burden light and the yoke easy.

With kindest greetings to Mrs. Hoover, in which Mrs. Macy and Miss Thomson join me, I am, with sincere esteem,

Faithfully yours,

Helen Keller.

Helen Keller listening to a "talking book" phonograph record with her fingertips, ca. 1944

Helen Keller was not able to perceive the spoken word but could tactually perceive sound vibrations.

[*I guess my only bad habit is robbing banks.*

ATTRIBUTED TO JOHN DILLINGER, BANK ROBBER WHO WAS PROCLAIMED
"PUBLIC ENEMY NUMBER ONE" IN JUNE 1934

From June 1933 through July 1934, John Dillinger and his gang led a crime spree throughout the midwest that made a mockery of local, state, and Federal law enforcement authorities. For more than a year, Dillinger stayed steps ahead of police and Federal agents in a brazen series of robberies, gunfights, and jail breaks. And although more than 10 victims died violently in the wake of his exploits, the public was captivated by a desperado who relished his own success in eluding "the greatest manhunt in U.S. history."

The pursuit of John Dillinger and the embarrassment it brought to Federal authorities transformed the Justice Department's Bureau of Investigation (later called the FBI) into a modern, well-oiled law enforcement machine that could effectively coordinate with every police department in the nation to fight crime. On July 22, 1934, Federal agents tracked and shot down Dillinger outside the Biograph movie theater in Chicago.

Rumors, legends, and myths persist regarding the preservation of anatomical specimens of John Dillinger; they are completely unfounded.

**Arrest photographs of
John Dillinger, January 1934**

RECORD GROUP 65, RECORDS OF THE
FEDERAL BUREAU OF INVESTIGATION

CAPIAS

JUN 11

D. C. FORM NO. 52

District Court of the United States

Northern DISTRICT OF Indiana

Hammond DIVISION

THE PRESIDENT OF THE UNITED STATES OF AMERICA

To the Marshal for the Northern *District of* Indiana —GREETING:

YOU ARE HEREBY COMMANDED that you apprehend JOHN DILLINGER, alias JOHN HALL, alias JOHN DONOVAN HALL, alias CLARENCE CRUSE, alias JOSEPH J. HARRIS, alias J.H. DONOVAN, alias KIRTLY (address unknown)

and him, on the first Mon day of November, 1934, have before the United States District Court for the Northern District of Indiana at

Hammond, Indiana to answer unto an

Indictment for vio: Motor Theft

contrary to the form of the statute in such case made and provided, and against the peace, government, and dignity of the United States of America.

Pursuant to statutes therefor provided, bail in the amount of Twenty-five thousand Dollars ($ 25,000.00) may be given in guaranty for the appearance of the aforesaid JOHN DILLINGER, ETC.,

at the time and place above stated. Failing therein, the aforesaid

JOHN DILLINGER, ETC., is to stand committed to some common jail in this district,

and the jailer thereof is hereby commanded to receive the body of the aforesaid

JOHN DILLINGER, ETC., and him safely keep to be dealt with according to law.

Hereof you are not to fail at your peril, and have you then and there this writ.

WITNESS, the Honorable Thomas W. Slick

United States District Judge at Hammond, Indiana

this the 11th day of June, A. D. 1934

MARGARET LONG

Clerk.

By *Helen Sweeney*

Deputy Clerk.

13—699

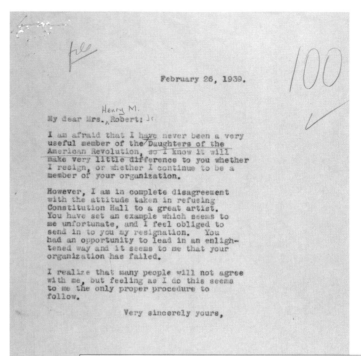

Eleanor Roosevelt, wife of President Franklin D. Roosevelt, was First Lady for 12 years. An outspoken advocate of social justice, she became a moral force during the Roosevelt administration, using her position as First Lady to promote social causes.

In a dramatic and celebrated act of conscience, Eleanor Roosevelt resigned from the Daughters of the American Revolution (DAR) when it barred the world-renowned singer Marian Anderson, an African American, from performing at its Constitution Hall in Washington, DC. (The DAR had adopted a rule excluding African American artists from the Constitution Hall stage in 1932 following protests over "mixed seating," blacks and whites seated together, at concerts of African American artists.) Following this well-publicized controversy, the Federal Government invited Anderson to sing at a public recital on the steps of the Lincoln Memorial. On Easter Sunday, April 9, 1939, some 75,000 people came to hear the free recital. The incident put both the artist and the issue of racial discrimination in the national spotlight.

View of 75,000 people gathered to hear the recital by Marian Anderson at the steps of the Lincoln Memorial, Easter Sunday, April 9, 1939

RECORD GROUP 306, RECORDS OF THE U.S. INFORMATION AGENCY (306-NT-965B-4) AP/WIDE WORLD PHOTOS

[*I am not surprised at Mrs. Roosevelt's action because she seems to me to be one who really comprehends the true meaning of democracy.*

MARIAN ANDERSON, CONCERT ARTIST, REFERRING TO MRS. ROOSEVELT'S RESIGNATION FROM THE DAUGHTERS OF THE AMERICAN REVOLUTION (DAR), FEBRUARY 28, 1939

AIRRAID ON PEARL HARBOR. THIS IS NO DRILL.

MESSAGE FROM COMMANDER IN CHIEF OF THE PACIFIC FLEET
TO ALL SHIPS IN THE HAWAIIAN AREA, DECEMBER 7, 1941

PSNY 3-7-41 25M — U. NAVAL AIR STATION, KODIAK ALASKA
Original — NAVAL COMMUNICATIONS

Heading	NPG NR 63 F L Z F5L 071830 C8Q TARI 0 BT
From:	CINCPAC	Date	7 DEC 41
To:	ALL SHIPS PRESENT AT HAWAIIN AREA.
Info:	- URGENT -

DEFERRED unless otherwise checked | ROUTINE.......... | PRIORITY.......... | AIRMAIL.......... | MAILGRAM..........

AIRRAID ON REARLHARBOR X THIS IS NO DRILL

07014

RM 58 1910 7DEC

Comdg Off	Exec	Comm	Oper	Supply	Disb	Med'l	Aerog	Pers	Pub Wks	Mar Det	A & R	Files	FAD	NRAB	OOD	WDO		

A—Denotes action   I—Denotes information   X—Denotes copy only

**Radiogram reporting the
Pearl Harbor attack,
December 7, 1941**

This urgent radio message
was issued by the Comman-
der in Chief of the Pacific
Fleet (CINCPAC) minutes
after the attack began.

RECORD GROUP 181, RECORDS OF
NAVAL DISTRICTS AND SHORE
ESTABLISHMENTS, NATIONAL
ARCHIVES AND RECORDS
ADMINISTRATION–ALASKA
REGION (ANCHORAGE)

On December 7, 1941, the U.S. naval base on the island of
Oahu, Hawaii, was subject to an attack that was one of the
greatest military surprises in the history of warfare. In less than
2 hours, the U.S. Pacific Fleet was devastated, and more than
3,500 Americans were either killed or wounded. The Japanese
attack on Pearl Harbor catapulted the United States into World
War II.

The American people were outraged. Though diplomatic
relations between the United States and Japan were deteriorat-
ing, they had not yet broken off at the time of the attack.
Instantly, the incident united the American people in a massive
mobilization for war and strengthened American resolve to
guard against any future lapse of military alertness.

TO THE CONGRESS OF THE UNITED STATES:

Yesterday, December 7, 1941 -- a date which will live in infamy -- the United States of America was suddenly and deliberately attacked by naval and air forces of the Empire of Japan.

The United States was at peace with that nation and, at the solicitation of Japan, was still in conversation with its Government and its Emperor looking toward the maintenance of peace in the Pacific. Indeed, one hour after Japanese air squadrons had commenced bombing in Oahu, the Japanese Ambassador to the United States and his colleague delivered to the Secretary of State a formal reply to a recent American message. While this reply stated that it seemed useless to continue the existing diplomatic negotiations, it contained no threat or hint of war or armed attack.

It will be recorded that the distance of Hawaii from Japan makes it obvious that the attack was deliberately planned many days or even weeks ago. During the intervening time the Japanese Government has deliberately sought to deceive the United States by false statements and expressions of hope for continued peace.

The attack yesterday on the Hawaiian Islands has caused severe damage to American naval and military forces. Very many American lives have been lost. In addition American ships have been reported torpedoed on the high seas between San Francisco and Honolulu.

- 3 -

With confidence in our armed forces -- with the unbounding determination of our people -- we will gain the inevitable triumph -- so help us God.

I ask that the Congress declare that since the unprovoked and dastardly attack by Japan on Sunday, December seventh, a state of war has existed between the United States and the Japanese Empire.

Franklin D. Roosevelt

THE WHITE HOUSE,
December 8, 1941.

**President Franklin D. Roosevelt's address to Congress,
asking for a declaration of war against Japan,
December 8, 1941**

Page 1 and signature page

President Roosevelt's famous "Day of Infamy" speech was a call to arms. One day after the attack, Roosevelt expressed outrage at Japan and confidence in the "inevitable triumph" of the United States. On December 8 the United States declared war against Japan; on December 11 Germany and Italy declared war against the United States.

RECORD GROUP 46, RECORDS OF THE U.S. SENATE, REPRODUCED WITH THE PERMISSION OF THE U.S. SENATE

U.S.S. *Shaw* exploding
during the Japanese
raid on Pearl Harbor,
December 7, 1941

RECORD GROUP 80, GENERAL
RECORDS OF THE DEPARTMENT
OF THE NAVY, 1798–1947
(80-G-16871)

The Japanese invasion of the Philippines came within hours of the December 7, 1941, attack on Pearl Harbor. In less than 1 month, the capital city of Manila fell to the Japanese.

During the next 4 months, American and Filipino forces held the Bataan Peninsula on the main island of Luzon and the nearby island fortress Corregidor in a delaying tactic until reinforcements could arrive. It was a gallant but hopeless fight. With food and medical supplies all but exhausted and no real hope for relief, the U.S. and Filipino troops fought beyond their level of endurance. Overwhelmed by starvation and disease, they were defeated. On April 9, 1942, Maj. Gen. Edward P. King, Jr., surrendered the 78,000 men under his command on Bataan; on May 6, General Wainwright, commander of all forces on the Philippines, surrendered his troops on Corregidor, as well as those remaining on the other islands. The U.S. Army returned to the Philippines in October 1944 to begin the lengthy process of liberation.

> *It is with broken heart and head bowed in sadness but not in shame that I report . . . that I must today go to arrange terms for the surrender of the fortified Islands of Manila Bay-Corregidor.*
>
> GEN. JONATHAN WAINWRIGHT TO PRESIDENT FRANKLIN D. ROOSEVELT, MAY 6, 1942

"The March of Death," May 1942

The Filipino and American defenders of Bataan became prisoners of war when General King surrendered on April 9. They were forced on a 65-mile trek known as the "Bataan Death March" during which many prisoners were beaten, clubbed, beheaded, and bayoneted by their Japanese captors. Others dropped from sheer exhaustion. It is estimated that one in every 10 men who began the march died along the way.

A Marine Corps caption identified these prisoners as *(left to right)* Samuel Stenzler, Frank Spear, and James McD. Gallagher.

RECORD GROUP 127, RECORDS OF THE U.S. MARINE CORPS (127-N-114541)

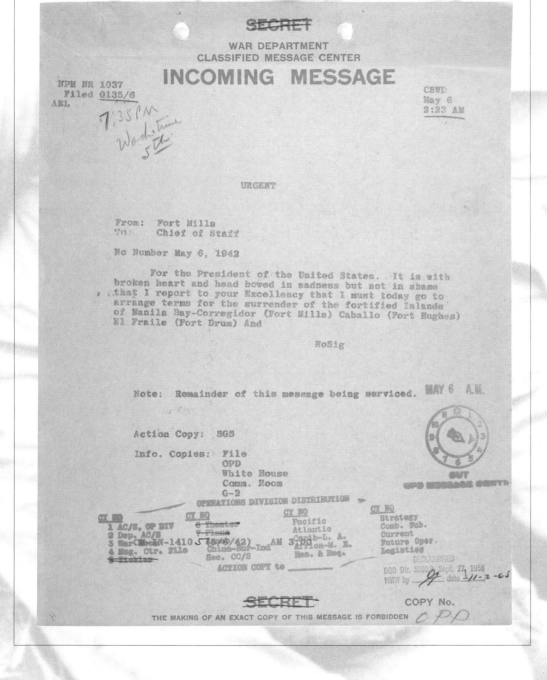

**Radiogram from Gen. Jonathan
M. Wainwright, commander of
U.S. Forces in the Philippines,
to President Franklin D. Roosevelt reporting his intent to
surrender Corregidor, May 6, 1942**

This is the last radiogram sent from
Corregidor before the surrender.
Communications were broken
before the final portion of the message could be received.

The President responded with
a message praising the general's
leadership and the "gallant struggle" of his men. Wainwright preserved that message throughout
the subsequent years of his captivity
in Japanese prison camps.

RECORD GROUP 165, RECORDS OF THE WAR
DEPARTMENT GENERAL AND SPECIAL STAFFS

"Birth of the Atomic Age," 1957

Painting by Gary Sheahan

This painting depicts the experiment that achieved the first controlled, self-sustaining nuclear chain reaction. No photographers were present.

Courtesy of the Chicago Historical Society

*E*ight months after the United States entered World War II, the Federal Government launched the Manhattan Project, an all-out, but highly secret, effort to build an atomic bomb— and to build one before the Germans did. The task was to translate the vast energy released by atomic fission into a weapon of unprecedented power. On December 2, 1942, a group of distinguished physicists, working under top-secret conditions in an unpretentious laboratory at the University of Chicago, took a crucial step toward this goal: they created the world's first controlled, self-sustaining nuclear chain reaction. Nobel prize-winning physicist Enrico Fermi directed the experiment.

We're Cookin!

RICHARD WATTS, PHYSICS STUDENT, RECORDING DATA AS THE WORLD'S FIRST CONTROLLED, SELF-SUSTAINING NUCLEAR CHAIN REACTION WAS ACHIEVED, DECEMBER 2, 1942

γ chamber		#3	#1	#6	
93 @ 10:55		.87	.01	.08	pause.
925	11.01	.85	.00	.07	
92	11.03	.84	.00	.065	
93	11.10	.84	.00	.06+	
925	11.13	.825	.00	.06	
925	11.14	.815	.00	.06	
925	11.15	.80	.00	.06	
92	11.20	.785	.00	.06	
92	11.23	.78	.00	.06	
	11.26		Rod pulled		
94	11.27	.96	.65	.69	
94	11.28	.965	.73	.76	
94	11.30	.965	.75	.81	
935	11.34	.91	.26	.28	
93	11.35	.86	.03	.10	
925	11.37	.84	.00	.06+	
92	11.39	.80	.00	.06	
915	11.40	.74	.00	.06	
91	11.40	.72	.00	.06	
91	11.45	.70	.00	.06	
91	11.49	.67	.00	.06-	
91	11.52	.66	.00	.06-	
91	12.00 Noon	.64	✓	✓	
90	12.02	.63	✓	✓	
895	12.06	.56	✓	✓	
89	12.08	.53	✓	✓	
89	12.09	.50	✓	✓	
	12.10	Rod IN			

γ chamber	Time	#3	#1	#6
.925	12.12 PM	.95	—	—
.93	12.13	.965	.93	.78
γ ×2(10⁴)		#3(10¹⁰)	#1(10¹⁰)	#6 ×2(10⁴)
—	2:21 PM	.97	.94	.99
—	2.23	.96	.905	.985
.945	2.34	.91	.84	.925
.94	2.40	.83	.67	.97
.94	2.49	.81	.62	.925
.935	2.57	.67	.38	.96
.92	3.03	.51	.14	.95-
.895	3.15	.20	0	.905
.875	3.26	.14	0	.895
.860	3.28	.09	0	.88
.850	3.29	.06	0	.87
	3.30	rod in		
.96	3.31	.95	.9	.99
.96	3.33	.97	.95	.995
.96	3.37	.955	.90	.99
.96	3.37	.935	.86	.99
.955	3.38	.91	.8	.99-
.95	3.38½	.87	.72	.98+
.94	3.39	.82	.61	.925
.94	3.39½	.74	.46	.97-
.93	3.40	.64	.18	.96-
.925	3.40½	.55	.16	.95
.92	3.41½	.48	.10	.94
.90	3.42½	.35	.02	.935-

※ We're Cookin!

**Notebook recording the first controlled, self-sustaining
nuclear chain reaction, December 2, 1942**

Fermi directed the construction of a pile of graphite and uranium bricks
and wooden timbers, assembled in the precise arrangement necessary to
start and stop a nuclear chain reaction. Cadmium rods inserted into the
pile regulated the nuclear reaction to prevent it from "burning" itself out
of control. Had it not been controlled, the experiment could have released
a catastrophic amount of energy, wreaking havoc in the middle of the
densely populated city of Chicago.

"We're cookin!" was the exuberant reaction recorded when the experiment succeeded *(right page, bottom left)*. The data shown here record the
nuclear reactor's response to the movement of the control rods.

RECORD GROUP 326, RECORDS OF THE ATOMIC ENERGY COMMISSION, NATIONAL ARCHIVES
AND RECORDS ADMINISTRATION–GREAT LAKES REGION (CHICAGO)

*If we were a primitive society,
movie stars would be gods.*

DIRECTOR SYDNEY POLLACK, 1994

Declaration of Intention (to become a U.S. citizen) of Greta Lovisa Garbo, September 9, 1948

RECORD GROUP 21, RECORDS OF DISTRICT COURTS OF THE UNITED STATES, NATIONAL ARCHIVES AND RECORDS ADMINISTRATION–PACIFIC REGION (LAGUNA NIGUEL)

Two decades after the first film studio was established in Hollywood, California, the American film industry entered its golden age. By the late 1930s studios were churning out hundreds of feature films each year. While the magic of the movies drew millions of people into the nation's theaters, the power and opportunity of the industry itself drew talent from around the world. Many of Hollywood's brightest stars—producers, writers, directors, and actors—hailed from other countries. In many instances, records documenting their immigration to the United States are preserved among the records of the National Archives.

Cary Grant, 1947

RECORD GROUP 208,
RECORDS OF THE OFFICE
OF WAR INFORMATION
(208-PU80-F3)

Petition for Naturalization of Archibald Alexander Leach, better known as Cary Grant, June 26, 1942

RECORD GROUP 21, RECORDS OF DISTRICT COURTS OF THE UNITED STATES, NATIONAL ARCHIVES AND RECORDS ADMINISTRATION–PACIFIC REGION (LAGUNA NIGUEL)

61

UNITED STATES OF AMERICA

PETITION FOR NATURALIZATION

No. 98061

[...]erson, under Sec. 310(a) or (b), 311 or 312, of the Nationality Act of 1940 (54 Stat. 1144-1145)]

(A)

[...]STRICT Court of THE U.S. at LOS ANGELES, CALIF.

[...], hereby made and filed pursuant to Section 310(a)(4)(b), or Section 311 or 312, of the Nationality Act of 1940, respectfully shows:

[...] name is ARCHIBALD ALEXANDER LEACH (CARY GRANT)

[...]esidence is 1038 Ocean Front, Santa Monica, Calif. My occupation is Actor

[...]years old. (5) I was born on Jan. 18, 1904 in Bristol, England

[...]scription is as follows: Sex M; color wh, complexion dark, color of eyes bro, color of hair blk, height 6 feet 1½ inches, [...] pounds; visible distinctive marks; race white; present nationality Great Britain

[...]rried; the name of my wife was Virginia Cherrill we were married on Feb. 9, 1934

[...]on, England; or she was born at Carthage, Ill. on April 12, 1908

[...]ered the United States at on for permanent residence in the United States, and now resides at

London, England and was naturalized on

certificate No.; or became a citizen by birth in U.S.
(7a) (If petition is filed under Section 311, Nationality Act of 1940) I have resided in the United States in marital union with my United States citizen spouse for at least 1 year immediately preceding the date of filing this petition for naturalization.
(7b) (If petition is filed under Section 312, Nationality Act of 1940) My husband or wife is a citizen of the United States, is in the employment of the Government of the United States, or of an American institution of research recognized as such by the Attorney General of the United States, or an American firm or corporation engaged in whole or in part in the development of foreign trade and commerce of the United States, or a subsidiary thereof; and such husband or wife is regularly stationed abroad in such employment. I intend in good faith to take up residence within the United States immediately upon the termination of such employment abroad.

(8) I have no children; and the name, sex, date and place of birth, and present place of residence of each of said children who is living, are as follows:

(9) My last place of foreign residence was Bristol, Somerset, England (10) I emigrated to the United States from Bristol England (11) My lawful entry for permanent residence in the United States was at New York under the name of Archibald Alex Leach on July 28, 1920 on the SS Olympia as shown by the certificate of my arrival attached to this petition.
(12) Since my lawful entry for permanent residence I have not been absent from the United States, for a period or periods of 6 months or longer, as follows:

DEPARTED FROM THE UNITED STATES			RETURNED TO THE UNITED STATES		
PORT	DATE (Month, day, year)	VESSEL OR OTHER MEANS OF CONVEYANCE	PORT	DATE (Month, day, year)	VESSEL OR OTHER MEANS OF CONVEYANCE

(13) (Declaration of intention not required) (14) It is my intention in good faith to become a citizen of the United States and to renounce absolutely and forever all allegiance and fidelity to any foreign prince, potentate, state, or sovereignty of whom or which at this time I am a subject or citizen, and it is my intention to reside permanently in the United States. (15) I am not, and have not been for the period of at least 10 years immediately preceding the date of this petition, an anarchist; nor a believer in the unlawful damage, injury, or destruction of property, or sabotage; nor a disbeliever in or opposed to organized government; nor a member of or affiliated with any organization or body of persons teaching disbelief in or opposition to organized government. (16) I am able to speak the English language (unless physically unable to do so). (17) I am, and have been during all of the periods required by law, attached to the principles of the Constitution of the United States and well disposed to the good order and happiness of the United States. (18) I have resided continuously in the United States of America for the term of 1 year, at least immediately preceding the date of this petition, to wit: since 7/28/20 (19) I have not heretofore made petition for naturalization

number on at in the

Court, and such petition was dismissed or denied by that Court for the following reasons and causes, to wit: and the cause of such dismissal or denial has since been cured or removed.
(20) Attached hereto and made a part of this, my petition for naturalization, are a certificate of arrival from the Immigration and Naturalization Service of my said lawful entry into the United States for permanent residence (if such certificate of arrival be required by the naturalization law), and the affidavits of at least two verifying witnesses required by law.
(21) Wherefore, I, your petitioner for naturalization, pray that I may be admitted a citizen of the United States, and that my name be changed to CARY GRANT

(22) I, aforesaid petitioner, do swear (affirm) that I know the contents of this petition for naturalization subscribed by me, that the same are true to the best of my own knowledge, except as to matters therein stated to be alleged upon information and belief, and that as to those matters I believe them to be true, and that this petition is signed by me with my full, true name: SO HELP ME GOD.

Archibald Alexander Leach

U. S. DEPARTMENT OF JUSTICE
IMMIGRATION AND NATURALIZATION SERVICE
Form N-406
(Edition of 1-9-41)

A note, in case of failure, by Gen. Dwight D. Eisenhower, June 5, 1944, but misdated July 5

On December 7, 1943, President Roosevelt informed Gen. Dwight D. Eisenhower that he would command *Operation Overlord.* Six months later, having directed the massive preparations for D-day and given the final order setting it all in motion, General Eisenhower wrote this note, preparing for the possible failure of the operation, and placed it in his wallet. He praised the men he commanded and accepted total responsibility for its failure. In reviewing this document in 1966, Eisenhower attributed the mistaken date to "careless error."

OK, let's go.

Gen. Dwight D. Eisenhower giving the final order for D-day, the assault on Nazi-occupied France, June 5, 1944

The greatest amphibious attack the world has ever seen was the Allied invasion of Nazi-occupied France during World War II. Its codename was *Operation Overlord,* and it was launched on June 6, 1944, D-day. It was a miracle of coordination as vast bureaucracies assembled thousands of troops, ships, and aircraft in the south of England to prepare for the cross-Channel invasion. The ultimate purpose was to eliminate Nazism by striking at the heart of Germany's war machine. The operation was a striking success: by the end of D-day, some 156,000 Allied troops had breached the Nazis' "Atlantic Wall," which the leader of the Third Reich, Adolf Hitler, had thought impregnable.

Transcription

Our landings in the Cherbourg-Havre area have failed to gain a satisfactory foothold and I have withdrawn the troops. My decision to attack at this time and place was based upon the best information available. The troops, the air and the Navy did all that Bravery and devotion to duty could do. If any blame or fault attaches to the attempt it is mine alone.—July 5

"Landing on the coast of France under heavy Nazi machine
gun fire are these American soldiers, shown just as they
left the ramp of a Coast Guard landing boat"
Photograph by CphoM. (Chief Photographer's Mate)
Robert F. Sargent, June 6, 1944

RECORD GROUP 26, RECORDS OF THE U.S. COAST GUARD (26-G-2343)

> *In these papers the Nazis . . . convicted themselves of the most heinous crimes. . . .*
>
> JOURNALIST WILLIAM SHIRER, ON NAZI DOCUMENTS SEIZED
> BY THE ALLIED ARMIES AT THE END OF WORLD WAR II

During the 12 years of the Third Reich, from 1933 to 1945, the Nazi regime identified the European Jews as the priority enemy of Germany and targeted them for extermination during World War II. The "Final Solution" was the code name for the genocidal program in which six million Jews were murdered. Millions of other innocent men, women, and children—gypsies, handicapped, Poles, homosexuals, Jehovah's Witnesses, Soviet prisoners of war, and political dissidents—were also victims of mass murder in the horrific events known collectively as the Holocaust.

The Nazi government established a system of concentration camps in the 1930s to imprison those groups of people who represented a racial or political threat to Nazi authority. Some of the concentration camps became killing centers; others were labor camps where prisoners died of overwork, torture, starvation, or disease.

The National Archives and Records Administration holds one of the world's largest collections of Holocaust-related documents. They were captured by the Allies and used as evidence in war crimes trials held at Nuremberg and elsewhere. Ironically, some of the most compelling evidence of Nazi atrocities was created by the Nazis themselves.

"Lublin Murder Camp, one of the storehouses for clothing taken from the victims. This one contained over one million pairs of shoes," 1945

At the Nazi death camps, the murders and looting of victims' property were executed with military precision. Everything taken from the victims—clothing, shoes, jewelry, and cash—was carefully sorted and recycled into the German war effort.

RECORD GROUP 208, RECORDS OF
THE OFFICE OF WAR INFORMATION
(208-AA-132H-33)

Totenbuch Mauthausen (Mauthausen Death Book),
August 8, 1940–March 26, 1942

Although the deaths of most Holocaust victims went unrecorded, the Mauthausen concentration camp in upper Austria maintained a death ledger in a set of 7 volumes that covers the period from January 1939 to April 1945. Of the estimated 199,404 prisoners who passed through the Mauthausen concentration camp, it is believed that 119,000 died. The volumes list 35,518.

These pages show an entry number, national or ethnic origin, prisoner number, name, date and place of birth, cause of death, and date and time of death of 27 people. Of the 27 prisoners listed here, 26 were identified as Jews, 1 as a Pole. The cause of death was attributed, most often, to various medical ailments, although the last column on the right, reserved for "remarks," documents the deaths of prisoners "shot while attempting to escape" and "suicide [by jumping] in the quarry."

Record Group 238, National Archives Collection of World War II War Crimes Records

HQ
U.S. FORCES EUROPEAN THEATER

STAFF MESSAGE CONTROL

S E C R E T

OUTGOING MESSAGE

R O U T I N E

S E C R E T

```
TO              : AGWAR

FOR INFORMATION : US GROUP CONTROL COUNCIL

FROM            : US FORCES, EUROPEAN THEATER MAIN SIGNED EISENHOWER

REF NO          : S-21742    CITE: ETGEC    TOO: 060930B
```

1. Among the materials captured by U.S.Army and presently in custody of Commanding General, US Forces European Theater, are items such as:

    a. 300 pounds precious and semi-precious stones;
    b. 700 pounds of rings (gold and other metal);
    c. 3000 pounds of novelty jewelry;
    d. 3500 pounds of watches;
    e. 650 pounds of gold and silver tooth fillings obtained from BUCHENWALD;
    f. 4500 pounds of scrap metal (much of it believed to be silver)
    g. 18000 pounds of tableware (knive, forks, etc); and other quantities of materials such as watch cases and eye glass frames believed to contain precious metals.

2. This headquarters estimates that following technically trained personnel needed to appraise value of these materials:

    a. Two experts capable of appraising secondhand jewelry and unset precious and semi-precious stones;
    b. Two experts on reclaimed precious and semi-precious metals.

3. Request you ascertain from Treasury Department whether Bureau of Customs or other branch of the Treasury can make available personnel qualified to make on-the-spot appraisal of these materials. If so, arrange for departure of personnel in question at earliest possible date and notify this headquarters of expected date of arrival.

```
ORIGINATOR      : G-5            AUTHENTICATION: C L ADCOCK
                                               Brig Gen
INFORMATION     : SGS    G-
                  AG RECORDS     COORDINATED WITH: C/S
```

```
SMC DECLASSIFIED  6 Sept 45   0935 B   GHP/rc      REF NO: S-21742
E.O. 11652, Sec. 3(E) and 5(D) or (E)             TOO: 060930B
FS MEMO 11472                                     COPY NO
By _____ NARS, Date 8/22/74    S E C R E T
THE MAKING OF AN EXACT COPY OF THIS MESSAGE IS FORBIDDEN
```

Message from Gen. Dwight D. Eisenhower, U.S. supreme commander of the Allied Expeditionary Force, reporting on Nazi looted material captured by the U.S. Army, September 6, 1945

In April 1945 the U.S. Army discovered a huge cache of Nazi-looted gold and other valuables hidden in an abandoned potassium mine in the village of Merkers. The cache included $238.5 million worth of gold (equivalent to $2 billion today) and major art collections; but it is the items listed here— the jewelry, silverware, and dental work—that are the most poignant remnants of the Nazi victims.

RECORD GROUP 338, RECORDS OF THE U.S. ARMY COMMANDS, 1942–

"German loot from Buchenwald atrocity victims," May 21, 1945
Photograph by T4C (Technician, 4th Class) Roberts

Gold jewelry and other gold items belonging to the victims were melted down into gold bars and added to the German Reichsbank's gold reserves. Wristwatches were collected and used as Christmas gifts to Nazi military officials.

RECORD GROUP 111, RECORDS OF THE OFFICE OF THE CHIEF SIGNAL OFFICER (111-SC-206406)

In 1996, in response to the efforts of the World Jewish Congress, the U.S. Government launched a broad search into the fate of the property of the victims of Nazism, including Swiss bank accounts opened by Jews to protect their assets from the Nazis; heirs of those who died in the concentration camps were denied access to the accounts for lack of a death certificate. National and international interest grew quickly regarding Holocaust-era assets issues, including the financing of the Nazi German regime and war effort. More than a thousand researchers have been drawn to the National Archives, probing a wide range of topics related to Nazi looting and the economic warfare of World War II. Among the researchers are survivors of the Holocaust, or their heirs, seeking evidence in their quest for restitution or compensation.

> *The trouble is, there was blood on this gold, was there not?*
>
> U.S. PROSECUTOR THOMAS J. DODD CROSS-EXAMINING NAZI MINISTER OF ECONOMICS AND PRESIDENT OF THE REICHSBANK WALTHER FUNK, AT THE NUREMBERG WAR CRIMES TRIAL, MAY 7, 1946

> *It's hell to be President of the Greatest Most Powerful Nation on Earth.*
>
> HARRY S. TRUMAN, DIARY, NOVEMBER 5, 1950

arry S. Truman became President on April 12, 1945, in the final days of World War II. Thrust into office on the death of Franklin D. Roosevelt, Truman readily took on the responsibilities of the Presidency. While his candor and lack of pretense led to characterizations of him as "simple" and "ordinary," he assumed leadership of a nation that emerged from history's bloodiest conflict as the greatest power on earth. He presided over an uneasy transition from wartime to peace and made decisions that drove American politics and foreign affairs for the next half century.

The private papers of Harry S. Truman consist of diaries, memoranda, and letters—more than 1,300 to Mrs. Truman alone. They compose a lively, revealing record of the President's views on topics ranging from world affairs to fashion.

MONDAY, OCTOBER 31, 1949 — 304th Day — Hallowe'en—Reformation Day — 61 Days to come

from opposite page.

Irving—Barnett takes the plate and butter plates. John comes in with a napkin and silver crumb tray—there are no crumbs but John has to brush them off the table anyway. Barnett bring me a plate with a finger bowl and doyle on it. I remove finger bowl and doyle and John puts a glass saucer and a little bowl on the plate. Barnett brings me some chocolate custard. John bring me a demitasse (at long a little cup of coffee—about two good gulps) and my dinner is over. I take a hand bath in the finger bowl and go back to work.

What a life!

TUESDAY, NOVEMBER 1, 1949 — 305th Day — All Saints' Day — 60 Days to come

I have another hell of a day. Look at my appointment list. It is only a sample of the whole year. Trying to make the 81st Congress perform is and has been worse than cussing the 80th. A President never loses prestige fighting Congress. And I can't fight my own Congress. There are some terrible chairmen in the 81st. But so far things have come out fairly well. I've kissed and petted more consarned S.O.B. so-called Democrats and left wing Republicans than all the Presidents put together. I have very few people fighting my battles in Congress as I fought F.D.R.s

Had dinner by myself tonight. Worked in the Lee House office until dinner time. A butler came in very formally and said "Mr. President dinner is served." I walk into the dining room in the Blair House. Barnett in tails and white tie pulls out my chair, pushes me up to the table. John in tails and white tie brings me a fruit cup. Barnett takes away the empty cup. John brings me a plate, Barnett brings me a tenderloin, John brings me asparagus, Barnett brings me carrots and beets. I have to eat alone and in silence in a candle lit room—

opposite page.

OPPOSITE PAGE:

Diary of President Harry S. Truman, November 1, 1949

Truman's personal diaries record not only the historic events of his Presidency but the everyday occurrences of his life. Here, for example, he gives a complete account of an evening when the President of the United States dined alone.

Truman's wife Bess and daughter Margaret were at the center of his life, and he endured their absences with difficulty. There is wry humor and a touch of melancholy in this account of a dinner served to him at Blair House, where the First Family resided during a major White House renovation. Beneath all the pomp and splendor he describes—the grand, ceremonial trappings of the Office he revered—there is the simple, inescapable fact of Truman's humanity: he ate his dinner in silence and was lonely for the people he loved.

NATIONAL ARCHIVES AND RECORDS ADMINISTRATION,
HARRY S. TRUMAN LIBRARY, INDEPENDENCE, MISSOURI

TRANSCRIPTION

ENTRY BEGINS ON THE RIGHT SIDE OF THE
VOLUME AND CONTINUES ON THE LEFT

Had dinner by myself tonight. Worked in the Lee House office until dinner time. A butler came in very formally and said "Mr. President, dinner is served." I walk into the dining room in the Blair House. Barnett in tails and white tie pulls out my chair, pushes me up to the table. John in tails and white tie brings me a fruit cup. Barnett takes away the empty cup. John brings me a plate, Barnett brings me a tenderloin, John brings me asparagus, Barnett brings me carrots and beets. I have to eat alone and in silence in candle lit room. I ring—Barnett takes the plate and butter plates. John comes in with a napkin and silver crumb tray—there are no crumbs but John has to brush them off the table anyway. Barnett brings me a plate with a finger bowl and doily on it—I remove finger bowl and doily and John puts a glass saucer and a little bowl on the plate. Barnett brings me some chocolate custard. John brings me a demitasse (at home a little cup of coffee—about two good gulps) and my dinner is over. I take a hand bath in the finger bowl and go back to work.

What a life!

[*And you know, my friends, there comes a time when people get tired of being trampled over with the iron feet of oppression.*

MARTIN LUTHER KING, JR., DECEMBER 2, 1955

O n December 1, 1955, during a typical evening rush hour in Montgomery, Alabama, a 42-year-old woman took a seat on the bus on her way home from the Montgomery Fair department store where she worked as a seamstress. Before she reached her destination, she quietly set off a social revolution when the bus driver instructed her to move, and she refused. Rosa Parks, an African American, was arrested that day for violating the laws requiring racial segregation of public buses.

Mrs. Parks was not the first person to be prosecuted for violating the segregation laws on the city buses. However, she was a woman of unchallenged character, who was held in high esteem by all those who knew her. Her arrest became a rallying point around which the African American community organized a boycott of the buses in protest of the discrimination they had endured for years. Martin Luther King, Jr., the 26-year-old minister of the Dexter Avenue Baptist Church, emerged as a leader during the well-coordinated, peaceful boycott that lasted 381 days and captured the world's attention.

For her quiet act of defiance that resonated throughout the world, Rosa Parks is known and revered as the "Mother of the Civil Rights movement."

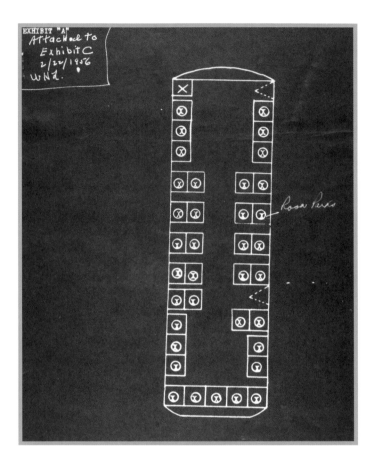

Diagram of the bus showing where Rosa Parks was seated on December 1, 1955

On the city buses of Montgomery, Alabama, the front 10 seats were permanently reserved for white passengers. This diagram shows that Mrs. Parks was seated in the first row behind those 10 seats. When the bus became crowded, the bus driver instructed Mrs. Parks and the other three passengers seated in that row, all African Americans, to vacate their seats for the white passengers boarding. Eventually, three of the passengers moved, while Mrs. Parks remained seated. J.F. Blake, the bus driver, believed he had the discretion to move the line separating black and white passengers. The law was actually somewhat murky on that point, but when Mrs. Parks defied his orders, he called the police.

RECORD GROUP 21, RECORDS OF DISTRICT COURTS OF THE UNITED STATES, NATIONAL ARCHIVES AND RECORDS ADMINISTRATION–SOUTHEAST REGION (ATLANTA)

🐦 *The documents shown here relating to Mrs. Parks's arrest are copies that were submitted as evidence in the* Browder v. Gayle *case.*

Fingerprint chart of Rosa Parks, December 1, 1955

Police officers Day and Mixon promptly arrested Mrs. Parks and took her to the police station, where she was booked, fingerprinted, and briefly incarcerated. The police report shows that she was charged with "refusing to obey orders of bus driver." For openly challenging the racial laws of her city, she remained at great physical risk while held by the police, and her family was terrified for her. When she called home, she spoke to her mother, whose first question was "Did they beat you?"

After Mrs. Parks was convicted, her lawyer filed a notice of appeal. On June 4, 1956, while her appeal was tied up in the state courts, a panel of three Federal judges ruled that racial segregation of the buses was unconstitutional. The U.S. Supreme Court upheld that decision on November 13, 1956.

RECORD GROUP 21, RECORDS OF DISTRICT COURTS OF THE UNITED STATES, NATIONAL ARCHIVES AND RECORDS ADMINISTRATION–SOUTHEAST REGION (ATLANTA)

Rosa Parks, 1950s

COURTESY OF THE PHOTOGRAPHS AND PRINTS DIVISION, SCHOMBURG CENTER FOR RESEARCH IN BLACK CULTURE, THE NEW YORK PUBLIC LIBRARY, ASTOR, LENOX AND TILDEN FOUNDATIONS

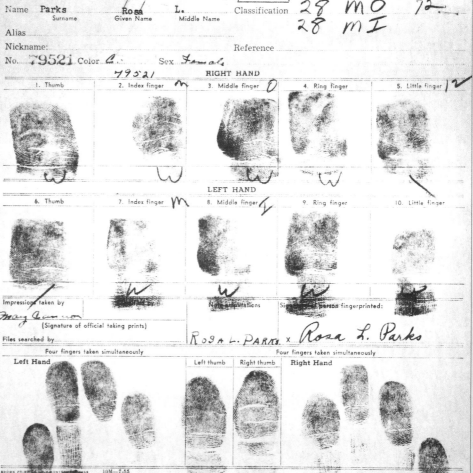

Inauguration of John Fitzgerald Kennedy, January 20, 1961

RECORD GROUP 111, RECORDS OF THE OFFICE OF THE CHIEF SIGNAL OFFICER (111-SC-578830)

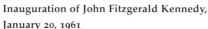

The inaugural ceremony is a defining moment in a President's career, and no one knew this better than John F. Kennedy as he prepared for his own inauguration of January 20, 1961. He wanted his address to be short and clear—devoid of partisan rhetoric and focused on foreign policy. He began constructing the speech in late November, working from a speech file kept by his secretary and soliciting suggestions from friends and advisors. While his colleagues submitted ideas and drafts, clergymen provided lists of biblical quotations. The final product, however, was distinctly the work of Kennedy himself. Aides recount that every sentence was worked, reworked, and reduced. It was a meticulously crafted piece of oratory that dramatically announced a generational change in the White House and called on the nation to combat "tyranny, poverty, disease, and war itself."

It was better than mine.

JOHN F. KENNEDY, COMPARING THE INAUGURAL ADDRESS OF THOMAS JEFFERSON TO HIS OWN, JANUARY 19, 1961

John F. Kennedy's handwritten draft of his inaugural address, January 17, 1961
Page 8 of 9 pages

Kennedy wrote his thoughts in his nearly indecipherable longhand on a yellow legal pad. The climax of the speech and its most memorable phrase, "Ask not what your country can do for you—ask what you can do for your country," was honed down from a thought about sacrifice that Kennedy had long held in his mind and had expressed in various ways in campaign speeches.

TRANSCRIPTION

Ask not what your country is going to do for you—ask what you can do for your country—my fellow citizens of the world—ask not what America or others will do for you—Ask rather what you can do [or] give for freedom. Ask of us—the same high standards of sacrifice and strength of heart and mind that we seek from you.

FROM THE SPEECH, AS DELIVERED JANUARY 20, 1961:

And so, my fellow Americans: ask not what your country can do for you— ask what you can do for your country.

My fellow citizens of the world: ask not what America will do for you, but what together we can do for the freedom of man.

Finally, whether you are citizens of America or citizens of the world, ask of us here the same high standards of strength and sacrifice which we ask of you. With a good conscience our only sure reward, with history the final judge of our deeds, let us go forth to lead the land we love, asking His blessing and His help, but knowing that here on earth God's work must truly be our own.

[*If I've lost Cronkite, I've lost middle America.*

PRESIDENT LYNDON B. JOHNSON, FOLLOWING WALTER CRONKITE'S STATEMENT
CRITICIZING U.S. POLICY IN VIETNAM, FEBRUARY 28, 1968

By the beginning of 1968, 7 years after the United States became seriously committed to the defense of South Vietnam against Communist North Vietnam, the number of U.S. troops in the conflict had peaked at 500,000; American casualties (dead, wounded, and missing) had reached 130,000. President Johnson's decision to escalate the war had all but derailed his agenda for the Great Society programs and his Presidency.

On January 30, 1968, the North Vietnamese launched the Tet Offensive, a coordinated attack hitting targets throughout South Vietnam, including the U.S. Embassy in Saigon. Although it failed in its main objectives of toppling the South Vietnamese government and crippling the military, it dealt a death blow to American public support of Johnson's war policies. By the time Walter Cronkite, one of the nation's best-known and most respected journalists, broadcast his criticism of American policy in Vietnam, President Johnson was forced to admit defeat in the arena of American public opinion. On March 31, 1968, President Johnson addressed the nation, simultaneously announcing a limit to the war in Vietnam and his decision to withdraw from politics.

President Johnson listens to a tape recording of an account of action in Vietnam made by his son-in-law Marine Capt. Charles Robb, July 31, 1968
Photograph by Jack Kightlinger

By late 1967, President Johnson had tentatively decided that he would not seek re-election in 1968. In January he asked former White House aide Horace Busby to draft a statement to that effect, but it was not until the final days of March that Johnson moved toward a final decision not to run.

NATIONAL ARCHIVES AND RECORDS ADMINISTRATION, LYNDON BAINES JOHNSON LIBRARY, AUSTIN, TEXAS (B1274-16)

cannot stand.

There is division in the American house now. Holding the trust that is mine -- as President of all the people -- I cannot disregard the peril in which that division could place the progress of the *American* people or the prospects of peace for all peoples. With *America's* ~~your~~ sons in the field far away, with *America's* ~~your~~ future in the balance here at home, ~~the~~ the American Presidency should be -- must only be -- used as an office of unity.

Believing this as I do -- and as I have for all the years I have served the public trust -- I have concluded that I shall not involve the Presidency *partisan* ~~that have~~ ~~deeply in,~~ developing in in the ~~divisions~~ of this political year. Accordingly,

Would
I shall not seek -- and ~~will~~ not accept -- the nomination of my party for another term as your President.

Sixty four months and ten days ago, in a moment of tragedy and trauma, the duties of this office fell upon me. I asked then for "your help and God's" that we might continue America on its course, binding up our wounds, healing our history, moving forward in new unity to clear the American agenda and to keep the American commitment for all our people.

We have kept that commitment -- and enlarged it. Through all time to come, America will be a stronger nation, a more just society, a land of greater opportunity and fulfillment for what we have done.

Draft of President Johnson's address to the nation announcing steps to limit the war in Vietnam and his decision not to seek re-election, March 31, 1968

Selected pages

For 30 minutes, on the evening of March 31, President Johnson spoke to the nation about Vietnam, announcing his orders to halt the bombing in areas inhabited by almost 90 percent of the North Vietnamese population. Within days, Hanoi responded positively to this first step toward peace by agreeing to negotiate.

Johnson then stunned the nation by announcing that he would not seek re-election (even his Cabinet officers had been notified only moments earlier). He later wrote that he wanted to demonstrate to the enemy and to the American people that his efforts to seek peace in Vietnam were "serious and sincere" and would not be tainted by considerations of partisan politics.

These pages, part of Horace Busby's handwritten first draft of the speech, show President Johnson's revisions.

NATIONAL ARCHIVES AND RECORDS ADMINISTRATION, LYNDON BAINES JOHNSON LIBRARY, AUSTIN, TEXAS

In Event of Moon Disaster

MEMO CONTAINING A STATEMENT FOR THE PRESIDENT TO MAKE TO THE AMERICAN
PEOPLE IN CASE OF DISASTER DURING THE *Apollo 11* MISSION, JULY 18, 1969

In the late 1950s the United States watched the Soviet Union take the lead in the rapidly escalating space race. The Soviet lead was both embarrassing and menacing to a nation that prided itself on technological know-how. On May 25, 1961, President John F. Kennedy challenged the nation to landing a man on the Moon before the end of the decade. The effort enlisted 20,000 companies, hundreds of thousands of individuals, and some $25.5 billion.

Eight years later, Edwin (Buzz) Aldrin and Neil Armstrong, astronauts of the *Apollo 11* Mission, became the first human beings to set foot on the Moon. It was a stunning achievement that boosted American confidence and prestige worldwide. More than 30 years later, the mission's success seems inevitable; but the great risks of the endeavor required that the administration prepare for the worst-case scenario.

-2-

Others will follow, and surely find their way home. Man's search will not be denied. But these men were the first, and they will remain the foremost in our hearts.

For every human being who looks up at the moon in the nights to come will know that there is some corner of another world that is forever mankind.

PRIOR TO THE PRESIDENT'S STATEMENT:

The President should telephone each of the widows-to-be.

AFTER THE PRESIDENT'S STATEMENT, AT THE POINT WHEN NASA ENDS COMMUNICATIONS WITH THE MEN:

A clergyman should adopt the same procedure as a burial at sea, commending their souls to "the deepest of the deep," concluding with the Lord's Prayer.

To   :   H. R. Haldeman

From: Bill Safire   July 18, 1969.

IN EVENT OF MOON DISASTER:

Fate has ordained that the men who went to the moon to explore in peace will stay on the moon to rest in peace.

These brave men, Neil Armstrong and Edwin Aldrin, know that there is no hope for their recovery. But they also know that there is hope for mankind in their sacrifice.

These two men are laying down their lives in mankind's most noble goal: the search for truth and understanding.

They will be mourned by their families and friends; they will be mourned by their nation; they will be mourned by the people of the world; they will be mourned by a Mother Earth that dared send two of her sons into the unknown.

In their exploration, they stirred the people of the world to feel as one; in their sacrifice, they bind more tightly the brotherhood of man.

In ancient days, men looked at stars and saw their heroes in the constellations. In modern times, we do much the same, but our heroes are epic men of flesh and blood.

Statement for the President to read in case the astronauts were stranded on the Moon, July 18, 1969

Unbeknownst to the American people, one of the President's senior advisers and speechwriters, William Safire, was asked to write a statement that the President would make to the American people in the event of a disaster. This memo to the President's chief of staff includes Safire's poignant tribute praising the courage and sacrifice of the astronauts. According to the memo, NASA would, at some point, cut off communications, leaving the astronauts to starve to death or end their own lives. As in a burial at sea, the souls of the astronauts would be commended "to the deepest of the deep."

NATIONAL ARCHIVES AND RECORDS ADMINISTRATION, NIXON PRESIDENTIAL MATERIALS PROJECT

OPPOSITE PAGE:

"Close-up view of an astronaut's leg and foot and footprint in the lunar soil," July 20, 1969

Photograph by Neil Armstrong

RECORD GROUP 306, RECORDS OF THE U.S. INFORMATION AGENCY (306-PSD-69-3133C)

Edwin (Buzz) Aldrin on the Moon, July 20, 1969

Photograph by Neil Armstrong

In this photograph, Armstrong and the *Eagle,* the lunar landing module, are reflected in Aldrin's visor helmet.

Of all the dangers of the Moon voyage, the one most feared by officials at NASA was that Aldrin and Armstrong would be stranded on the Moon— that the *Eagle* would be unable to get back up into orbit to rejoin the command capsule and the mission's third crew member, Michael Collins.

RECORD GROUP 306, RECORDS OF THE U.S. INFORMATION AGENCY (306-PS-69-3087/C)

> *You won't believe this, but the King is here.*
>
> AIDE OF PRESIDENT NIXON ANNOUNCING ELVIS PRESLEY'S UNEXPECTED
> ARRIVAL AT THE WHITE HOUSE, DECEMBER 21, 1970

AmericanAirlines

In Flight…

Altitude;

Location;   *0*

Dear Mr. President.
First I would like to introduce myself.
I am Elvis Presley and admire you
and Have Great Respect for your
Office. I talked to Vice President
Agnew in Palm Springs 3 weeks and
expressed my Concern for our Country.
The Drug Culture, The Hippie Elements,
The SDS, Black Panthers, etc do not
consider me as their enemy or as they
call it the Establishment. I call it America and

AmericanAirlines

In Flight…

Altitude;

Location;   *5*

~~approach~~
approach. I would Love to
meet you just to say hello if
you're not to Busy.
                Respectfully
                Elvis Presley

P.S. I believe that you Sir
were one of the Top Ten Outstanding Men
of America also.
I have a personal gift for you also
which I would like to present to you
and you can accept it or I will keep it
for you until you can take it.

On the morning of December 21, 1970, Elvis Presley approached the northwest gate of the White House and requested a meeting with President Nixon. He wanted to offer his services as a Federal agent in the war on drugs. The appearance of the legendary superstar, dressed in a dark, crushed velvet outfit, set off a flurry of memos and meetings as Nixon's button-down staff decided what to do. At 12:30 p.m., Presley was ushered into the Oval Office and the President met the "King."

It was an unlikely episode, filled with irony and contradictions. The "King of Rock and Roll," who had never entered the political arena, embraced the nation's highest elected official, whose taste in music favored the classical. The star, who later would be hospitalized for drug detoxification, asked to join the ranks of Federal agents fighting illegal drugs. Following his meeting with the President, Presley received a badge and certification as a "Special Assistant" of the Bureau of Narcotics and Dangerous Drugs.

Letter from Elvis Presley to President Nixon, December 21, 1970

Page 1 and signature page

Fleeing the protected isolation of his life as a super-star, Presley boarded an American Airlines flight from Los Angeles to Washington, DC, in the company of just one bodyguard. While in flight, he wrote this letter, asking to meet with the President "today, tonight or tomorrow." Citing his influence and popularity with America's youth, he asked to be made a "Federal Agent at Large" to help combat the nation's drug problem.

After landing in Washington, Presley completed this letter and personally delivered it to the visitor's kiosk at the White House gate.

NATIONAL ARCHIVES AND RECORDS ADMINISTRATION, NIXON PRESIDENTIAL MATERIALS PROJECT

President Nixon and Elvis Presley meet at the White House, December 21, 1970

Photograph by Ollie Atkins

Of the millions of photographs preserved by the National Archives, this is one of the most requested.

NATIONAL ARCHIVES AND RECORDS ADMINISTRATION, NIXON PRESIDENTIAL MATERIALS PROJECT (NLNP- 5364.18)

[

They got us.

During the night of June 17, 1972, five burglars broke into the offices of the Democratic National Committee at the Watergate office complex in Washington, DC. Investigation into the break-in exposed a trail of abuses that led to the highest levels of the Nixon administration and ultimately to the President himself. President Nixon resigned from office under threat of impeachment on August 9, 1974.

The break-in and the resignation form the boundaries of the events we now know simply as "Watergate." For 2 years public revelations of wrongdoing inside the White House convulsed the nation in a series of confrontations that pitted the President against the media, executive agencies, the Congress, and the Supreme Court. The Watergate affair was a national trauma—a constitutional crisis that tested and affirmed the rule of law.

The five burglars caught inside the Watergate complex and the two men who led the team, E. Howard Hunt and G. Gordon Liddy, were indicted on September 15, 1972. The items shown on the opposite page were presented as evidence during their trial.

THE WHITE HOUSE
WASHINGTON

August 9, 1974

Dear Mr. Secretary:

I hereby resign the Office of President of the United States.

Sincerely,

Richard Nixon

11.35 AM

The Honorable Henry A. Kissinger
The Secretary of State
Washington, D.C. 20520

HK

Richard M. Nixon's letter resigning the Presidency, August 9, 1974

On the morning of August 9, 1974, the day following President Nixon's televised resignation speech, White House Chief of Staff Alexander Haig presented this letter to President Nixon to sign. The President's resignation letter is addressed to the Secretary of State, in keeping with a law passed by Congress in 1792. The letter became effective when Secretary of State Henry Kissinger initialed it at 11:35 a.m.

RECORD GROUP 59, GENERAL RECORDS OF THE DEPARTMENT OF STATE

Address book of Watergate burglar Bernard Barker, discovered in a hotel room at the Watergate Hotel, June 18, 1972

This address book lists "HH," initials for Howard Hunt, and his telephone number at the "WH" or White House. Hunt was a White House consultant. After confirming that the telephone number listed here was indeed at the White House, the FBI linked the Watergate break-in to the White House during the investigation's earliest hours.

RECORD GROUP 21, RECORDS OF DISTRICT COURTS OF THE UNITED STATES

One of the $100 bills carried by the burglars during the break-in

Immediately before the break-in, Liddy distributed $100 bills to the burglary team to use as bribes in case they were caught. The discoloration of this bill was caused by a substance used during the investigation to detect fingerprints.

RECORD GROUP 21, RECORDS OF DISTRICT COURTS OF THE UNITED STATES

Chap Stick tubes with hidden microphones

E. Howard Hunt and G. Gordon Liddy, who led the Watergate break-in team, were stationed in a Watergate Hotel room while the burglary was underway. A lookout was posted across the street at the Howard Johnson Hotel. During the break-in, they would remain in contact with each other and with the burglars by radio. These Chap Stick tubes outfitted with tiny microphones were discovered in Hunt's White House office safe.

RECORD GROUP 21, RECORDS OF DISTRICT COURTS OF THE UNITED STATES

The "Cold War" is the term for the rivalry between the two blocs of contending states that emerged following World War II. It was a series of confrontations and tests of wills between the non-Communist states, led by the United States and Great Britain, and the Communist bloc, led by the Soviet Union, that lasted 45 years and, at one point, drew the world to the brink of nuclear war.

In August 1961 the Soviets erected the Berlin Wall to stop the mass exodus of people fleeing Soviet East Berlin for West Berlin and the non-Communist world. The wall was a mass of concrete, barbed wire, and stone that cut into the heart of the city, separating families and friends. For 28 years, it stood as a grim symbol of the gulf between the Communist East and the non-Communist West. In 1989 the Berlin Wall fell, signalling the end of the Cold War.

Mr. Gorbachev, open this gate.
Mr. Gorbachev, tear down this wall.

PRESIDENT RONALD REAGAN AT THE BRANDENBURG GATE
IN BERLIN, JUNE 12, 1987

One of President Reagan's speech cards from his remarks in Berlin, June 12, 1987

Twenty-six years after the construction of the Berlin Wall, as tensions between the two superpowers eased, President Ronald Reagan made a historic appearance at the Brandenburg Gate. He spoke passionately about the advance of human liberty and challenged Soviet leader Mikhail Gorbachev to "tear down this wall"—the ultimate symbol of Communist suppression—and to demonstrate a commitment to profound change.

NATIONAL ARCHIVES AND RECORDS ADMINISTRATION, RONALD REAGAN LIBRARY, SIMI VALLEY, CALIFORNIA

- 10 -

THERE IS ONE SIGN THE SOVIETS CAN MAKE THAT WOULD BE UNMISTAKABLE, THAT WOULD ADVANCE DRAMATICALLY THE CAUSE OF FREEDOM AND PEACE.

GENERAL SECRETARY GORBACHEV, IF YOU SEEK PEACE — IF YOU SEEK PROSPERITY FOR THE SOVIET UNION AND EASTERN EUROPE — IF YOU SEEK LIBERALIZATION: COME HERE, TO THIS GATE.

MR. GORBACHEV, OPEN THIS GATE.

MR. GORBACHEV, TEAR DOWN THIS WALL.

I UNDERSTAND THE FEAR OF WAR AND THE PAIN OF DIVISION THAT AFFLICT THIS CONTINENT — AND I PLEDGE TO YOU MY COUNTRY's EFFORTS TO HELP OVERCOME THESE BURDENS. TO BE SURE, WE IN THE WEST MUST RESIST SOVIET EXPANSION. SO WE MUST MAINTAIN DEFENSES OF UNASSAILABLE STRENGTH. YET WE SEEK PEACE. SO WE MUST STRIVE TO REDUCE ARMS ON BOTH SIDES.

President Ronald Reagan, Berlin, Germany, June 12, 1987

QUOTATION SOURCES

LISTED BELOW ARE THE SOURCES FOR QUOTATIONS THAT DO NOT COME DIRECTLY FROM THE DOCUMENT SHOWN.

PAGE 12. Whitman, Walt. *The Complete Poetry and Prose of Walt Whitman.* Vol. 2 (New York: Pellegrini & Cudahy, 1948) p. 402.

PAGE 14. Carruth, Gorton and Eugene Ehrlich, editors. *American Quotations* (New York: Wings Books, 1994) p. 511.

PAGE 18. Inscription on the Main Post Office, New York City, adapted from Herodotus, ca. 484 B.C.

PAGE 20. Freeman, Douglas Southall. *George Washington: A Biography,* Vol. 3, *Planter and Patriot* (New York: Charles Scribner's Sons, 1951) p. 440.

PAGE 22. Randall, William Sterne. *Benedict Arnold–Patriot and Traitor* (New York: William Morrow and Company, Inc., 1990) p. 564.

PAGE 25. Kaminski, John P. and Gaspare J. Saladino, editors. *The Documentary History of the Ratification of the Constitution.* Vol. XVIII, *Commentaries on the Constitution: Public and Private, Volume 6, 10 May to 13 September 1788* (Madison, Wisconsin: State Historical Society of Wisconsin, 1995) p. 266.

PAGE 26. Letter from Gen. Horatio Gates to President Thomas Jefferson, July 18, 1803, National Archives and Records Administration, RG 59, General Records of the Department of State, Applications and Recommendations for Office, Jefferson, under Smith, Col. Wm.

PAGE 28. *The Journals of Lewis and Clark.* Edited and Introduction by Frank Bergon (New York: Viking, 1989) entry of November 7, 1805.

PAGE 30. From "The Star-Spangled Banner," verse by Francis Scott Key, inspired by the bombardment of Fort McHenry, September 14, 1814.

PAGE 32. McKissack, Patricia and Frederick L. *Rebels Against Slavery: American Slave Revolts* (New York: Scholastic Press, 1996) p. 125.

PAGE 36. Stegner, Wallace. *The Gathering of Zion: The Story of the Mormon Trail* (New York: McGraw-Hill Book Company, 1964) p. 6.

PAGE 38. Dillon, Richard. *Fool's Gold: The Decline and Fall of Captain John Sutter of California* (New York: Coward-McCann, Inc., 1967) p. 278.

PAGE 40. *John Brown's Raid.* U.S. National Park Service, National Park Service History Series, Superintendent of Documents No. 129-2:J61/4, Washington, DC, 1974, p. 60.

PAGE 42. Davis, William C. *A Government of Our Own, The Making of the Confederacy* (New York: Random House, 1986) p. 125.

PAGE 45. Freeman, Douglas Southall. *R.E. Lee: A Biography,* Vol. 1 (New York: Charles Scribner's Sons, 1935) p. 475.

PAGE 46 (title quote). *Freedom – A Documentary History of Emancipation, 1861–1867,* Series II, *The Black Military Experience.* Edited by Ira Berlin. Associate Editors: Joseph P. Reidy, Leslie S. Rowland (Cambridge: Cambridge University Press, 1982) p. 582.

PAGE 46 (1st paragraph). Sandburg, Carl. *Abraham Lincoln—The War Years,* Vol. II (New York: Harcourt, Brace & Company, 1930) p. 240.

PAGE 46 (2nd paragraph). Bates, David Homer. *Lincoln in the Telegraph Office—Recollections of the United States Military Telegraph Corps during the Civil War,* Introduction by James A. Rawley (Lincoln, Nebraska: University of Nebraska Press, 1995) p. 141. (originally published New York: Century Co., 1907).

PAGE 49 (2nd paragraph). Catton, Bruce. *Never Call Retreat. The Centennial History of the Civil War,* Vol. 3 (Garden City, New York: Doubleday & Company, Inc., 1965) p. 416.

PAGE 49 (3rd paragraph). Sherman, William Tecumseh. *Memoirs of Gen. W.T. Sherman, Written by Himself,* Vol. II (New York: Charles L. Webster & Co., 1891) p. 111.

PAGE 50 (title quote). Donald, David Herbert. *Lincoln* (New York: Simon & Schuster, 1995) p. 550.

PAGE 50 (1st paragraph). Oates, Stephen B. *With Malice Toward None—The Life of Abraham Lincoln* (New York: Harper & Row, Publishers, Inc., 1977) pp. 425–426.

PAGE 54. *Frederick Douglass on Women's Rights Contributions in Afro-American and African Studies,* Number 25, Edited by Philip S. Foner (Westport, CT: Greenwood Press, 1976) p. 159.

PAGE 56. Brown, Dee. *Bury My Heart at Wounded Knee: An Indian History of the American West* (New York: Henry Holt and Company, 1970) p. 122.

PAGE 58. Shiels, Archie W. *The Purchase of Alaska* (University of Alaska Press, 1967) p. 182.

PAGE 60. *An Account of the Proceedings on the Trial of Susan B. Anthony* (published in Rochester, NY, 1874) p. 152.

PAGE 62. Dyer, Frank Lewis and Thomas Commerford Martin. *Edison—His Life and Inventions* (New York and London: Harper & Brothers, 1910) p. 607.

PAGE 66. Fox, Stephen. *John Muir and His Legacy: The American Conservation Movement* (Boston: Little, Brown and Company, 1981) p. 12.

PAGE 68. Liliuokalani. *Hawaii's Story by Hawaii's Queen* (Rutland, Vermont: Charles E. Tuttle Company, 1979) p. 373.

PAGE 70. Sinclair, Upton. *The Autobiography of Upton Sinclair* (New York: Harcourt, Brace & World, Inc., 1962) p. 126.

PAGE 72. University of Louisville. Accessed June 14, 2000. http://www.spd.louisville.edu/~j0hard01/MaidenVoyage.html.

PAGE 74. Tompkins, Frank (Col.). *Chasing Villa: The Story Behind the Story of Pershing's Expedition into Mexico* (Harrisburg, PA: The Military Service Publishing Company, 1934) p. 214.

PAGE 78. Kennan, George F. *Soviet-American Relations 1917–1920*, Vol. I, *Russia Leaves the War* (Princeton, New Jersey: Princeton University Press, 1985) p. 154.

PAGE 82 (title quote). Clemens, Samuel Langhorn. *Mark Twain's Autobiography*, Vol. 2. Introduction by Albert Paine (New York: Harper & Brothers, 1924) p. 297.

PAGE 82 (1st paragraph). Keller, Helen. *The Story of My Life*. Introduction by Ralph Barton Perry (Garden City, New York: Doubleday & Company, Inc., 1954) p. 26.

PAGE 84. Girardin, G. Russell with William J. Helmer. *Dillinger—The Untold Story* (Bloomington and Indianapolis: Indiana University Press, 1994) p. 109.

PAGE 86. *New York Times*. "Mrs. Roosevelt Indicates She Has Resigned From DAR Over Refusal of Hall to Negro." February 28, 1939, p. 1.

PAGE 96. Basinger, Jeanine. *American Cinema—One Hundred Years of Filmmaking* (New York: Rizzoli International Publications, Inc., 1994) p. 74.

PAGE 98. Ambrose, Stephen E. *D-Day—June 6, 1944: The Climactic Battle of World War II* (New York: Simon & Schuster, 1994) p. 189.

PAGE 100. Shirer, William L. *The Nightmare Years: 1930–1940* (Boston: Little, Brown and Company, 1984) p. 638.

PAGE 103. *Trial of the Major War Criminals Before the International Military Tribunal, Nuremberg, 14 November 1945–1 October 1946. (The Blue Series)*, Vol. 13. (Nuremberg, Germany: International Military Tribunal, 1947–1949) pp. 178–79.

PAGE 104. President Truman's diary entry of November 5, 1950. National Archives and Records Administration, Harry S. Truman Library, President's Secretary Files, Diaries.

PAGE 106. Branch, Taylor. *Parting the Waters: America in the King Years, 1954–63* (New York: Simon & Schuster, 1988) p. 139.

PAGE 108. Parmet, Herbert S. *JFK: The Presidency of John F. Kennedy* (New York: The Dial Press, 1983) p. 82.

PAGE 110. Cronkite, Walter. *A Reporter's Life* (New York: Alfred A. Knopf, 1996) p. 258.

PAGE 116. Krogh, Egil (Bud). *The Day Elvis Met Nixon* (Bellevue, Washington: Pejama Press, 1994) p. 9.

PAGE 118. Emery, Fred. *Watergate—The Corruption of American Politics and the Fall of Richard Nixon.* (New York: A Touchstone Book Published by Simon & Schuster, 1994) p. 135.

ACKNOWLEDGMENTS

"American Originals" simply would not have happened without the participation of the entire staff of the National Archives and Records Administration. Bringing a selection of documents from the vaults and stacks throughout the National Archives system to our exhibit cases and, finally, to these pages, represents a multi-year, agency-wide effort. This work was supported by John W. Carlin, Archivist of the United States, and was completed under the direction of Michael J. Kurtz, Assistant Archivist for Records Services–Washington, DC; Edith M. James, director of Public Programs; and Christina Rudy Smith, chief curator of the Exhibits Staff.

The staff of the National Archives and Records Administration is made up of archivists, technicians, conservators, photographers, designers, editors, teachers, librarians, as well as specialists in other areas. They are the stewards of our documentary heritage. Their dedication and commitment to the mission of the National Archives make it a true privilege to work here.

On the Exhibits Staff, Michael Jackson designed five different versions of the exhibition installed in the Rotunda from 1995–2001, as well as the traveling exhibition; James D. Zeender was the exhibit registrar, safeguarding the documents throughout all phases of exhibit preparation; Darlene McClurkin assisted throughout the research and production phases in countless ways. In the Textual Archives Services Division, Michael E. Pilgrim, provided guidance, as well as physical access to many of the documents on an almost daily basis over many months. Catherine Nicholson of the Document Conservation Laboratory led all aspects of the conservation work; Earl McDonald, from Preservation Programs, photographed many of the documents reproduced in this book, and Steven T. Puglia, from the Special Media Preservation Laboratory, scanned the images in preparation for their publication. From the Product Development Staff, Nancy Mottershaw initiated and coordinated the entire publication process, Maureen MacDonald copyedited countless permutations of "American Originals" manuscripts and Serene Feldman Werblood designed this book. Susan Cooper of the Communications Staff has been an unflagging supporter of "American Originals" since its inception in 1993, and her suggestions have greatly enriched the exhibition and the book.

In the Washington, DC, area, I would like to thank the following staff members of the National Archives who lent their expertise, skills, and support time and again: George Briscoe, Marjorie Ciarlante, Milton O. Gustafson, Kenneth W. Heger, Walter Hill, Michael Meier, Michael Musick, James S. Rush, and Mitch Yockelson of the Textual Archives Services Division; Michael L. Gillette, Richard Hunt, Kenneth Kato, and Charles E. Schamel of the Center for Legislative Archives; Pat Anderson, David Mengel, and Karl Weissenbach of the Nixon Presidential Materials Staff; Kate Flaherty and Mary Ilario of the Special Media Archives Services Division; Norvell Jones, Susan Page, Barbara Jo Pilgrim, and Mary Lynn Ritzenthaler of the Document Conservation Laboratory; Cecelia Epstein and Richard Schneider of the Special Media Preservation Laboratory; Jeffrey Hartley of the Archives Library Information Center; Nancy Malan of the Office of Regional Records Services; Michelle Cobb and Douglas Thurman of the Office of Presidential Libraries; Bruce Bustard, Marilyn Paul, and Catherine Farmer of the Exhibits Staff; and those who came to the Exhibits Staff as part of their professional training: Merisue D'Achille, Tracee Butler, Bonnie Curtin, and Amy Patterson.

"American Originals" was drawn from the nationwide holdings of the National Archives. I owe a special debt of gratitude to those people who work outside the Washington metropolitan area. The directors and archivists of the regional archives and Presidential libraries, as well as the curatorial staffs of the museums within the libraries, came through time and again with suggestions for exhibit items, as well as all kinds of logistical and technical support. I would like to thank Alycia Vivona at the Franklin D. Roosevelt Library; Clay Bauske, Mark Beveridge, and Pauline Testerman at the Harry S. Truman Library; David Haight and Dennis Medina at the Dwight D. Eisenhower Library; Megan Desnoyers, Stephen Plotkin, and Maura Porter at the John Fitzgerald Kennedy Library; Claudia Anderson and Charleu Diercks at the Lyndon Baines Johnson Library; Jay Hakes and Sylvia Naguib at the Jimmy Carter Library; and Greg Cumming at the Ronald Reagan Library. I also thank the people at the Herbert Hoover and George Bush libraries who helped bring their treasures to "American Originals." In the Office of Regional Archives Services, James Owens, Northeast Region (Boston); Robert Morris, Northeast Region (New York City); Kellee Blake, Mid-Atlantic Region; Charles Reeves and Mary Ann Hawkins, Southeast Region; Peter Bunce and Donald Jackanicz, Great Lakes Region; Mark Corriston and Alan Perry, Central Plains Region; Kent Carter, Southwest Region; Eileen Bolger, Rocky Mountain Region; Sharon Roadway, Pacific Region (San Francisco); Diane Nixon, Pacific Region (Laguna Niguel); Susan Karren, Pacific Alaska Region (Seattle); and Thomas Wiltsey, Pacific Alaska Region (Anchorage).

Outside the National Archives, I would first like to thank Douglas Brinkley, Director of the Eisenhower Center for American Studies at the University of New Orleans, whose opening statement to this book reminds us of the power of original documents. I am greatly indebted to the scholars and experts throughout the nation who reviewed exhibit captions and portions of this manuscript. However, I would like to especially thank Stephen E. Ambrose, preeminent author and historian, for reading an early exhibit script and offering many invaluable suggestions. Kenneth Bowling, adjunct associate professor of history at the George Washington University and co-editor of *The Documentary History of the First Federal Congress, 1789–1791,* graciously read most of those portions of the script relating to the American Revolution and the creation of the Constitution. Wayne S. Cole, diplomatic historian, professor emeritus at the University of Maryland, and volunteer docent at the National Archives, reviewed every caption in "American Originals" that relates to American foreign affairs. Historians and park rangers at National Park Service historic sites across the United States have been extremely generous with both their time and wealth of knowledge. Leslie S. Rowland, co-editor of *Freedom: A Documentary History of Emancipation, 1861–1867,* drafted a portion of the text on the significance of the Emancipation Proclamation; and John Sellers, historian in the Manuscript Division of the Library of Congress, reviewed much of the text relating to Abraham Lincoln. Kurt Ritter, associate professor of Speech Communication, Texas A & M University, shared his research on President Reagan's speechwriting and reviewed captions on this topic. Elaine Olah, state records administrator of the New Mexico State Records Center and Archives, and Robert Torres, state historian of New Mexico, helped us to feature some of the oldest documents in the National Archives holdings. Jill Brett of the Library of Congress reviewed several exhibit scripts and made many improvements. I also thank Lee Williams, chief registrar of the Smithsonian Institution Traveling Exhibition Service (SITES), and Gregory E. Marcangelo of the Prints and Photographs Division of the Library of Congress. Finally, I thank Phil McCombs who has shared more great ideas for "American Originals" than could fit between the covers of any book.

"American Originals" has been a group effort. Nobody knows that better than I. It is impossible to name each of the hundreds of people who brought this project to completion, but I thank them all wholeheartedly.

Stacey Bredhoff, *Curator*